The
Best
SEX
for Life

DR PATRICIA WEERAKOON

Sexologist, therapist, best-selling author
of *Teen Sex By The Book*

Growing Faith
An imprint of
Anglican Youthworks
PO Box A287
Sydney South NSW 1235
Australia

Ph: +61 2 8268 3333
Fax: +61 2 8268 3357
Email: sales@youthworks.net
Website: www.cepstore.com.au

Published October 2013.

National Library of Australia
ISBN 978-1-925041-03-3

Managing editor—Julie Firmstone
Theological editors—Belinda Pollard, Marshall Ballantine-Jones
Cover and typesetting—Joy Lankshear
Illustrations—Lisa Flanagan

To my ever patient husband Vasantha:
We have gone from the diamond ring
to wedding band, had our share of
sexpectations, grown in sanctification and
reached our sexy 60s together. I thank God
for bringing you into my life.

*And to my son Kamal, my theological
consultant in all things sex:*
I couldn't have written this book without
your wisdom.

*Also to my lovely, vivacious and brilliant
editor, Julie:*
I have learned as much about writing from
you as you have learned about sex by reading
my manuscripts. Thank you for tolerating my
vagaries and brain snaps.

Contents

Introduction
Why a(nother) book on sex?

This is a Christian book about sex. I am a Christian sexologist. I have worked for over 25 years speaking, researching and teaching sex and relationships in Sri Lanka, America and Australia. This book is a distillation of my passion for good, healthy sex and my love for God.

This book is not an instruction book for Christians on how to be better lovers, although we do talk about this. Nor is it a detailed exegesis of biblical texts on sex and marriage, although we discuss that too. There are many books that do both of these well.[1]

This book will demonstrate that a Christ-centred, God-glorifying approach to your personal sexuality will be good for everyone: for you as an individual; for you as a married couple; and for your family, church, and society as a whole. It does this by bringing together sexological research, sexual biology and the Bible, to show how sex in marriage bonds a man and a woman in beautiful ways.

---

1   See the bibliography in Appendix 5.

If you are a couple, this book is for you. You may be engaged or newlywed. You may have a baby, or one or more children. Or else you may be an older couple with teenage kids, adult kids or no kids at all. You may even be in a retirement village. As long as you are part of a couple at some stage in your marital journey, read on.

It is important to realise that sex is an important part—but not the whole—of a Christian marriage. This book discusses sex and marriage in the context of God's purposes and patterns for relationships generally. Misunderstanding this relational context of sexuality has left contemporary society with a whole lot of confused, shallow, unsatisfying and unhealthy sexual expectations and practices. We will discuss and critique this from a biblical perspective.

I hope that reading this book will empower you to mould your relationships, both sexual and otherwise, in a way that builds you up as a couple and enables you to enjoy the best sex for life, as God intended.

Why is this book timely and important?

We live in a world of rampant individualism and self-fulfilment. We take for granted that everything we think, say and do has to benefit us, individually, in some way. And the ultimate self-fulfilment is, of course, sex. We take for granted that sexual satisfaction is a basic human right. And our culture vigorously affirms it. Magazines, media and billboards scream the mantra of sexuality as the panacea for all unhappiness. Television programs and the internet present sex as a commodity for entertainment. Pornographic sites and erotic novels invite us into fantasy worlds of deviant second-hand sexuality. Adult retail stores present extreme sexual behaviours as something to be tried and enjoyed.

If this is what we expect from our sex lives, then the image of one man and one woman, committed to living together and only having sex with each other for the rest of their lives, seems unnatural. Social trends indicate that marriage is an outdated institution. In Australia, the marriage rate (the number of marriages that occur for every 1000 residents) has fluctuated greatly over the years and in recent years has been the lowest on record.[2] The number of de facto relationships is increasing and about a third of marriages end in divorce. Articles[3] and books celebrate the joys of non-monogamy and negotiated infidelity.

All this has two effects on us. Firstly, it makes us dissatisfied. We think that our sex lives aren't what they should be. Sex is just not frequent enough, exciting enough or orgasmic enough compared with what we see on television or in movies, erotic books or on porn sites. Secondly, we tend to blame our spouse. They're not 'performing' for us, not satisfying us. Surely, there must be something better.

How might married couples deal with this?

Some do nothing and accept that 'this is as good as it gets' in a marriage relationship. They pretend to be satisfied, living in a state of relational tension while filling their life and mind with other activities and thoughts, sometimes even succumbing to sexual temptations like pornography or extramarital sex.

---

2   Weston, R & Qu, L 2013, 'Working out relationships' in *Australian Family Trends*, No. 3, viewed on June 8 2013, <http://www.aifs.gov.au/institute/pubs/factssheets/2013/familytrends/aft3/aft3.pdf>.
3   For example, <http://www.smh.com.au/lifestyle/life/i-believe-in-negotiated-fidelity-20130606-2nshf.html>.

Others struggle silently in ignorance. They realise that God intends them to enjoy deep, meaningful relationships and mutually fulfilling sex with each other, but they don't know what that actually means, or how to achieve it. They long to live out their married life, including their sexuality, God's way but have no idea where to go for information and guidance.

And then there are the couples who go looking for some exercise or technique to give them a fulfilling and happy sex life. Couples who take this route read books and visit websites that give instructions for how to be better communicators, lovers and spouses. They go to workshops. Sometimes these are Christian but mostly they are new-age sensuality seminars. Sometimes they consult a sex therapist. Couples follow the advice given, talk more, make date nights, and find their partner's 'love language'. They practise mindfulness, Tantra, yoga. And these work—for a while.

Most of these are not wrong in themselves. The trouble is they don't solve the real problem. They're just techniques that don't actually address our deep conceptions of who we are as sexual beings, and what sex is for. They give us a legalistic rule book rather than helping us to change our fundamental attitudes to ourselves and each other. And so, after a while, many couples find themselves back where they started, or even worse off for having tried to fix it by themselves. They are like actors on a stage, reading the script and going through the motions, but with no understanding of the true meaning or outcome of the play, and ignoring the scriptwriter and director. It may be fun and interesting for a little while but, without any deep sense of meaning and purpose, it's not going anywhere. It won't last.

When it comes to sex and relationships, we need to understand the scriptwriter's purpose and be willing to be guided by the director. We cannot do it by ourselves.

God is the Scriptwriter, Creator and Director of our lives. This includes our sex lives. If we accept this, we realise that the best way to have a happy, fulfilled sex life is to understand God's purpose for sexuality and be willing to live under biblical direction for our relationships in marriage and beyond.

To live this way we need to change from the inside out. We need to develop a new vision of our sexuality and a pattern of living that reflects the blessing of sex given to us by God. Sex is a wonderful and precious gift to be enjoyed in marriage and, like all parts of our lives, used to bring God glory. When we understand this, we forget about ourselves and our own personal pleasure. Our sexuality becomes a part of a life of other-focused loving. And when we approach our sexuality in this way—with the attitude that 'it's not about pleasing myself, but caring for, serving, and satisfying my spouse'—it leads to the best sex for both, for a lifetime.

So, for Christian couples to have a good sex life and relationship, we do not start with a magic box of techniques. We begin with an evangelical, theological understanding of sex: a perspective on what it means to be sexual and behave sexually, one that is soaked through with the gospel of Jesus Christ, God incarnate.

But wait. For some of you, sex does not seem like a gift or a blessing; rather, it seems like a curse! Some bear heavy loads of guilt and shame because of past sexual experiences. You may have had casual sex as a teenager, or been carried away by the hook-up culture of your peers. Maybe you pushed the boundaries of intimacy in your engagement period. You might be the victim of sexual abuse or broken sexual relationships. Others could be struggling with same-sex desires, even feeling uncomfortable with their gender. The burden of all this guilt and shame makes you want to hide. You may never have spoken with anyone about what you've been through, maybe not even your spouse. This is all the more reason to start with an evangelical theology of sex. The God who made us sexual, and who shows us how to behave in sexually healthy ways, is the same God who gave his one and only Son for us. Jesus did not come for the healthy, but for the sick; he did not come to call the righteous, but sinners (Matthew 9:12–13; Mark 2:17; Luke 5:31–32). Paul states with confidence, 'God demonstrates his own love for us in this: While we were still sinners, Christ died for us' (Romans 5:8). Remember the hymn, 'From heaven he came and sought her to be his holy bride; with his own blood he bought her and for her life he died'?[4] Jesus' blood cleanses every sin, including sexual sin.

This cleansing means both forgiveness for the mess we've made of our lives, and restoration to good, healthy ways of living—ways that are in line with God's purposes for us. This includes his purposes for making us as sexual beings. Having cleaned us up, God empowers us to live a new way of life. God wants to turn our lives around so that we can enjoy a lifetime of good sex according to his pattern. The change probably won't happen immediately. But it will—slowly, eventually—as the Holy Spirit makes us more and more like Jesus.

4   From 'The Church's One Foundation' by Samuel J. Stone, 1839–1900.

Finally, some of you may accept the world view that you cannot be a Christian and enjoy great sex. You may have bought the world's myth that the Bible is anti-sex and that all it says about sex is 'it's dirty—don't do it'. If this is you, you need this book most of all! Read on, and find out how delightful and wonderful the biblical view of sex is.

The book is in three parts. Part 1 is an overview of an evangelical theology of sexuality—sex according to God, Jesus and the Bible. In Part 2, we look at the body in all its wonderful, divinely designed structure and function. We'll see how living according to God's plan for sex is both pleasurable and good for us, because it agrees with the way our bodies operate. In Part 3, we'll explore what good sex looks like across the whole of your marriage. We'll look at four stages in married life: engagement; the newly married, child-free and extended-honeymoon years; children and a growing family; and mature, ageing adults. In each stage we will look at sexual biology, values and behaviour from the perspective of God's design for sex and relationships.

Whatever life stage you are at, this book is for you. Whether you've just slipped the engagement ring on your finger, or are exploring how to spend your time in retirement, I invite you to discover how living God's way leads to healthy, pleasurable sex and intimate, satisfying relationships at every stage of your walk as a couple.

This is a sex book. It directly addresses sensitive, personal issues. We will discuss the day-to-day activities of a good sex life plus hot topics like premarital sex, infidelity, pornography, sex aids (sex toys), sexual dysfunctions and variant sexual practices. I will also give you some guidelines on how you can have a more satisfying sex life as a Christian couple.

You will find that we talk about sexual activity as being between a man and a woman. Researchers tell us that about 2–3% of people of all ages have been, or are currently in, some form of same-sex relationship.[5] So while we'll acknowledge same-sex relationships, this book is written for the majority of people with heterosexual desires and practices.

You may find that reading this book raises more questions about sex than it answers. Or you may feel convicted of something that has happened in your sex life. In this case, talk to a mature Christian friend, a counsellor or your church pastor. There is no shame in asking for help. We worship a God who came to redeem every part of our lives.

Finally, while this is a book for couples, it is also for pastors, church leaders and counsellors. Our hope and prayer is that this book will empower you to join Christians everywhere in living our sex lives as God intends.

Be countercultural. We, as Christians, know the truth when it comes to married sex. Let us demonstrate this to a sex-obsessed world.

5   Chandra, A, Mosher, WD, Copen, C, & Sionean, C 2011,'Sexual behavior, sexual attraction, and sexual identity in the United States: Data from the 2006–2008 National Survey of Family Growth', *National Health Statistics Reports*, No. 36, Hyattsville, MD: National Center for Health Statistics. Viewed on April 6 2013 at <http://www.cdc.gov/nchs/data/nhsr/nhsr036.pdf>.

As the Apostle Peter said:

Dear friends, I urge you, as foreigners and exiles, to abstain from sinful desires, which wage war against your soul. Live such good lives among the pagans that, though they accuse you of doing wrong, they may see your good deeds and glorify God on the day he visits us. (1 Peter 2:11–12)

A Christian couple—one man and one woman, in love with each other, purposefully conforming their whole marriage relationship to God's biblical pattern—are a living, breathing, walking and talking gospel tract. In a world that prioritises the selfish gratification of desire, you will shine as a beacon of true sexual fulfilment found in the spouse to whom you have promised yourself, and ultimately, in God.

Part 1

A theology of biblical sexology

The Bible has a lot to say about sex and marriage. It starts with a romantic sexual relationship of a man and a woman in a lush garden. In the Song of Songs we see a book of erotic poetry—eight chapters of sensual loving between a husband and wife. Throughout the Bible, from Abraham and Sarah to Joseph and Mary, we see examples of intimate loving marriages.

God makes it very clear. We are sexual beings: man and woman, before God and each other. It is the way we are created. It applies to our body, brain and behaviour. And it is good. In fact God says it is *very good*.[6]

Let's go to where it all began—to the book of Genesis and the Garden of Eden with Adam and Eve. Having created the earth and all the plants and animals, God looked around and saw that it was all good. Well, not quite. Adam, the first male, was alone and God saw that this was *not good* (Genesis 2:18). So, God created Eve. Now we have man and woman.

> Then God said, 'Let us make mankind in our image, in our likeness, so that they may rule over the fish in the sea and the birds in the sky, over the livestock and all the wild animals, and over all the creatures that move along the ground'. So God created mankind in his own image, in the image of God he created them; male and female he created them. God blessed them and said to them, 'Be fruitful and increase in number; fill the earth and subdue it'. (Genesis 1:26–28a)

Here we see four aspects to God's plan for our sex life. God created men and women to be relational, embodied, sexual and purposeful. Let's look at each of these.

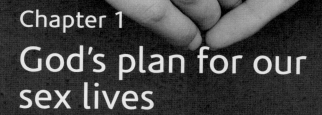

Chapter 1
God's plan for our sex lives

Created for relationships

Genesis 1:26 records God saying *'let us make mankind in our image'*. To bear God's image means that, as humans, we reflect the perfect, divine relationship of love in the Holy Trinity. The Father, Son and Holy Spirit show both unity and diversity in relating to one another. Jesus perfectly reflects God because he is the second person of the Trinity, the eternal Son of God, who came into the world as a man. As a man, he enjoyed a perfect relationship with the Father, by the power of the Spirit. He demonstrated that perfect relationship by obeying the Father's plan, which was for him to give his body as a sacrifice for sinners.

This shows us that God wants us to enjoy life-giving relationships of total intimacy, trust and honesty, because he is himself a relational, life-giving God. He is the epitome of relationship; as the Apostle John said, *God is love* (1 John 4:16). Out of his love, God made this universe as a place of abundant life. Real life—full, complete and valued—does not come just from feeding ourselves with physical pleasures like food and sex. Real life comes from having healthy relationships. This is why we're happiest when we feel loved and protected by other people.

God's love completes us 'vertically'. Our primary, life-giving relationship needs to be with the crucified and risen Jesus. Nothing and no-one else can be given first priority. To do so would be idolatry, and the whole Bible, both Old and New Testaments, condemns and mocks idolatry.

As people who are complete in Christ, we turn this vertical, divine love out 'horizontally': we love others as Christ loved us. We receive love from others. God puts us in families and communities where we can give and receive love. And in this rich exchange of love, we enjoy life.

Marriage is the closest and most personal human relationship possible. And sex is the most intimate act of human sharing that is physically possible in that relationship. So marriage is the core context where God calls us to live a life of outward-oriented, self-giving, other-serving love. And therefore, marriage is the best context in which to give each other satisfying, caring, fulfilling sex. Good sex isn't 'taken' from your spouse because you 'demand' it. You 'give' good sex to your spouse because you 'love' them—just like Jesus came, in love, to give us eternal life.

But it is important to realise that, while marital love, romance and sex are wonderful, marriage is not the only fulfilling relationship we can enjoy. Non-sexual friendships can be intimate, enriching and empowering. Ask any happy Christian single who is part of a vibrant Christian community.

Sex is wonderful, but a life without sex never killed anyone. Life without Jesus kills: it leads to eternal death. This is why our relationship with Jesus must come first. Otherwise, even good things like marriage and sex can degenerate into idolatry.

Created embodied: man and woman

At creation, God designed man and woman embodied: that is, to live, find identity and serve God in and through human bodies. This means that whatever happens to our bodies matters to God. Paul calls believers to 'honour God with your bodies' (1 Corinthians 6:20). This means every part, especially those parts treated with special modesty that are involved in sexual activity (1 Corinthians 12:21–23). God intended the sexual aspects of our bodies to operate so that a man and a woman would be able to enjoy excellent sex together. We can see this from reading both Genesis and Song of Songs. Song of Songs describes the man and his bride admiring each other's bodies, and enjoying great sex with each other, in a garden paradise as if they're an ideal Adam and Eve.

The couple in the Garden of Eden had a unique, complementary character and identity (Genesis 1:27). Adam and Eve were perfectly gendered as male and female: two discrete sexes, their bodies complementary in structure and function as God ordained. Adam and Eve would have been totally comfortable in their roles as man and woman. Adam knew he was a man and that Eve was a woman; Eve likewise knew she was a woman and Adam, a man. They were both totally content with that. They weren't stressed about who they were; they accepted themselves (their bodies and their identities) as God had made them.

Part of being embodied is being sexual. Let's hear what the Bible has to say about that.

Created as sexual beings

After the excitement of seeing each other comes sex between man and woman. The plans for this first marriage are clearly laid out in Genesis 2:24–25:

> *That is why a man leaves his father and mother and is united to his wife, and they become one flesh. Adam and his wife were both naked, and they felt no shame.*

Here is the gift of sex in the context of a man and woman in a marriage relationship. Sex is good—the whole Bible says so. Song of Songs is an entire book of erotic poetry. The book of Proverbs doesn't just say 'avoid adultery', it also encourages us to enjoy our marital partner (Proverbs 5:15–20). Paul advised the married couples in the Corinthian church not to deprive each other of sex, but to willingly give themselves to each other (1 Corinthians 7:2–5). He also warned Timothy that one characteristic of false teachers will be that they will try to prevent people from enjoying God's good gifts of food and sex (1 Timothy 4:3–5).

But God's blessings are fragile and need to be handled with care, according to the Creator's instructions. The goodness of sex is there to be enjoyed in God's designed purpose: within marriage between a man and a woman. Marriage, and sex within marriage, makes a man and a woman 'one flesh'—it unites the two genders of humanity together in wonderful, satisfying, pleasurable, productive and life-giving harmony. Jesus himself affirmed this created pattern when, in response to the Pharisees' question on divorce, he said:

> Haven't you read that at the beginning the Creator 'made them male and female', and said, 'For this reason a man will leave his father and mother and be united to his wife, and the two will become one flesh'? So they are no longer two, but one flesh. 'Therefore what God has joined together, let no-one separate.' (Matthew 19:4–6)

Paul also uses this 'one flesh-ness' of marriage as a metaphor for Christ and the Church (Ephesians 5:28–32). Our relationship with Christ is as intimate as that of husband and wife. In fact, we might even say it's more intimate because it's produced by the Holy Spirit and goes on forever. Paul's point is this: Christ willingly came to 'join' himself with his people, to become 'one' with us. Just like marriage and sex draw husband and wife into a deep, physical union that affects everything about them, and in which they share everything, so Christ and his people share a deep union that affects everything about us, and in which we share everything. Christ takes our sin and we get eternal life in him.

Let's explore some of the implications of this view of the role of sex within marriage.

- *Marriage is a covenant commitment*: Both the man and the woman leave their parental family to set up a new family together. In western society that's no big deal, because we think about ourselves as individuals. We may even feel that families are a pain in the neck, because they stop us doing what we want. But think about it: our parents have cared for us, nurtured us, and know all our good and bad points. Our parents (and brothers and sisters, if we have any) know us intimately. When a man and a woman get married, they are now going to care for, nurture and get to know each other intimately for the rest of their lives. This is why the Bible talks of marriage as a 'covenant'. Covenant is the word the Bible uses to describe the deepest possible personal commitment, where you give yourself completely to the good and welfare of the other person, without holding anything back.

- This uniting will be a *one-flesh* union. The unity will be more than the physical proximity of the bodily parts and sharing of body fluids in sexual intercourse. It will be one that connects the couple at a deeply emotional and even spiritual level—a metaphysical bonding of body, brain and spirit. The partners are in such a close relationship that they often think and feel and act as one. It will be sexual pleasure given as a gift of love, not taken as a right.

- It would be a *naked and no-shame* relationship: one of total and unabashed trust. To be naked before another person is to be ultimately vulnerable. And to feel no shame in this act of shared intimacy is an act of trust—a blatant sharing of the body and emotions. Each act of sex will be one where both husband and wife know that they will not be judged on the size and shape of their genitals, or their sexual performance in bed. It will not matter who initiates sex, whether they are both aroused, or if they orgasm. Sex will be an act where mutual vulnerability will be celebrated and supported, and the wrinkles of ageing and the associated slowdown in sexual function are lovingly accepted. There will be no shame because covenant love covers a multitude of flaws.

- Together in the marriage they will fulfil God's command to *procreate and rule* over the earth. This sometimes does not occur in marriage, either by choice or due to a fertility problem in one of the partners. Even in this situation, every act of sexual intercourse has the *potential for creation* of new life, and is enjoyed and celebrated as such.

Created for a purpose

God is a purposeful God. He is not random: he made the world, and humans, purposefully. As our Creator, he has the right to define what sex and marriage are for (their purpose).

We learn that humankind (man and woman) were created to rule over the earth and subdue it (Genesis 1:26, 28). As image bearers of God, man and woman were created to rule and not to *be ruled* by creation. By this means they were to keep the good order that God had created: that is, God –> humankind –> the rest of creation. They were to do this as a couple. In Genesis 1, we see God create the first humans, man and woman. Genesis 2 expands the story by telling us how he did so. God created man first and gave him the role of leader, and then created woman as the perfect and suitable helper and companion, for the task of ruling the world (as Genesis 2 puts it, cultivating the garden) and procreating for the future. The writer of Psalm 8 praised God for giving frail, insignificant humanity such an exalted position of cosmic rule. In all of this, God gives us several purposes for sexuality in marriage. Let's explore these.

It was not good for the man to be alone. We are not meant to be self-sufficient individuals; we need relationships. Marriage (including sex in marriage) is the most intimate human relationship possible. So, one purpose of marriage and sex is *relational fulfilment*.

Adam and Eve's unashamed nakedness, combined with the erotic descriptions in Song of Songs, shows that bodily beauty and sexual pleasure are good. *Physical pleasure* is another purpose of marital sex. And by creating man and woman as *complementary* humans, God placed the relational and physical joys of sex within heterosexual marriage.

As mentioned previously, marriage and sex are meant to produce babies. Sex is meant for *procreation*. It's an aspect of being outwardly focused and productive. God commanded humans to be fruitful and multiply (Genesis 1:28). Sex, love and productivity are bound together. Love brings a couple together; they enjoy love together; and their mutual love brings forth new life—children.

There is more to the outwardly-focused purpose of marriage. God did not simply make man and woman in his image: he appointed them as rulers of the world. Adam and Eve were not just made for each other; they were to tend the garden. Marriage and sex are 'private' in that they belong exclusively to the couple. The relational and sexual pleasures of marriage are meant to enable the married couple to engage in their other relationships, and their other responsibilities, with renewed vigour. In this sense, marriage is not 'private', but a 'public' institution: it affects the married couple's place in, and approach to, the rest of the world. Christian marriages *strengthen society*.

The most amazing purpose of marital sex is *evangelism*. Mutually caring, fulfilling, life-bringing sex between a man and a woman who have committed themselves to each other for life, points to the teachings of Jesus Christ. If a true biblical marriage is but the reflection of the relationship between Christ and his Church, it is a perpetual declaration of the gospel. This is why the Bible can use marriage as a metaphor for God and his people in both the Old and New Testaments. The virtues that characterise the gospel—other-focused care, commitment and sacrifice—demonstrate both the character of the Triune God himself, and the character of good sex in a healthy marriage.

And in all this, *sex honours God*. It is right and proper that we honour and thank God for giving us this good gift of sex. God wants us to use sex the proper way—his way—because he wants us to be happy and healthy. He is delighted when we conduct our sexuality so as to serve and care for each other, because that's how he wants his children to behave. The highest purpose of sex, which knits all the other purposes together, is to glorify God.

These purposes are not independent: they interlock and reinforce each other. This is why God's way works. When we conduct our sexuality in light of his purposes for sex, we can expect everything to work in a happy harmony that genuinely feels good because it *is* good, for everyone.

But of course, most of us aren't enjoying such perfect marital and sexual bliss. If you were, you probably wouldn't be reading this book! We live in a fallen world, where our relationships, bodies and desires have all been damaged because of the consequences of us rejecting God and trying to live independently of him. The next chapter looks at the havoc this creates in us, and also at what God has done in Christ to fix it.

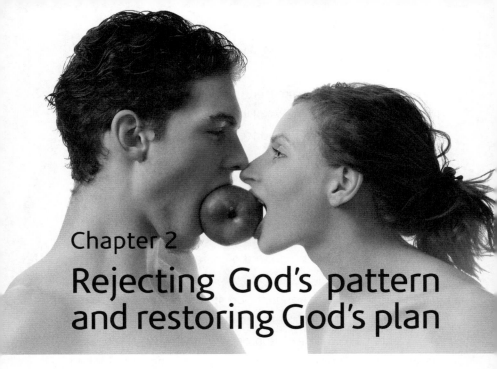

Chapter 2
Rejecting God's pattern and restoring God's plan

Rejecting God's pattern

The Bible really does turn everything upside down. What the world calls maturity, freedom and joy, the Bible considers slavery and death. What the Bible considers good and healthy, the world judges as foolish at best and downright evil at worst.

These days, this reversal of values is most obvious in the area of sexuality. According to God, healthy sexuality is characterised by conformity. He calls us to shape (to conform) our sexual lives to his pattern. The key to conforming to God's sexual pattern is to fit our sexuality (conform it) to our spouse's needs and desires. Biblically speaking, the thing most likely to destroy healthy sexuality is self-centredness.

What, according to contemporary western culture, characterises healthy sexuality? Independent, autonomous self-satisfaction, of course! That's a fancy way of saying: 'I' define what 'my' sexuality is and what it means for 'me' to be sexually satisfied, with no consideration for 'you' or anyone else in the universe, least of all God. We assume that sexual desire is the core of human existence. Therefore, the end goal of life becomes maximum satisfaction of our sexual desires. The only way to discover what our desires really are and how to satisfy them is to experiment, to try new things. How else are we going to grow and mature? So, change partners, change techniques, maybe even try it with the same gender, just to see what it's like. According to the world, nothing destroys healthy sexuality more than conforming yourself to someone else's demands.[7]

None of this is new. It goes back to our first parents—Adam and Eve. To live with God in his garden and enjoy themselves and everything else in God's presence, they needed to obey God and conform to his pattern for their lives. That conformity wasn't particularly difficult—all they had to do was not eat from one tree. But they refused to do that. They believed Satan's lie that God's commands were not good for them, and that his way of living was oppressive. They believed that rejecting God, and doing things their own way, was the way to real freedom and fulfilment. So they rejected God, made themselves independent of him, and we've been suffering the consequences ever since.

Adam and Eve fractured their relationship with God. Because that relationship is the most important one in the universe, that separation splintered everything else in their existence. Instead of absolute trust and safety, they became

---

7   The technical term for such conformity is heteronomy. Autonomy is self-legislation; heteronomy is other-legislation.

suspicious of and hostile towards each other. They used to delight in each other's bodies, in each other's gender, with all their sexual potential. Now they had become ashamed and frightened of each other's gaze. So they covered themselves up, hid from each other (Genesis 3:7) and from God (Genesis 3:10), and then passed on the blame (Genesis 3:12–13). God's judgement confirmed this mutual hostility. They were supposed to be complementary, mutually delighting in each other. From this point on there was conflict between them: 'your desire will be for your husband, and he will rule over you' (Genesis 3:16b).

Rejecting God also had physical consequences. Both man and woman were punished in their own way with 'hard labour'. They were supposed to procreate, to fill the earth. From here on Eve would give birth in pain (Genesis 3:16a). They were supposed to rule the earth together, cultivate the garden, be king and queen of all they surveyed. But the ground itself rebelled against Adam, producing thorns and thistles, and forcing him to work and sweat to get food. This hard labour eventually resulted in death, a return to the dust (Genesis 3:19). And seeing as they didn't really want to live with God, disobeying him and then hiding from him, he gave them what they wanted: he kicked them out of the garden (Genesis 3:23). To be outside the garden was to be cut off from life, to live under the shadow of death. The Apostle Paul draws both these images of 'hard labour' together when he says 'the whole creation has been groaning as in the pains of childbirth right up to the present time' (Romans 8:22). The whole world we live in, everything we consider 'normal'—including sex—has been damaged by sin.

So of course sex isn't as good as we want it to be. In this world, nothing is as good as we want it to be. In fact, nothing's as good as God himself created it to be. And that's because we've messed up everything by rejecting him. Sin damages all aspects of our sexuality, from our biology and body chemistry to our sexual ambitions and love-lives. Let's have a look at just a few examples.

As we said before, sex is for pleasure. That's one of its divinely intended purposes. The problem is that these days, we think that's all that sex is for—personal, individual gratification. So we organise our lives to serve this goal of maximising our immediate sexual pleasure. Anything that gives us that immediate sexual pleasure is good: masturbating to a pornographic video; solo sex with a sex toy or a blow-up doll. If you need a human, then a sex worker should do. They come without the hassles of a relationship. And they probably cost less in the long run anyway.

If we want some basic relationship with the person we're having sex with, but still want to be able to get rid of them when they become inconvenient, we might use a 'rent a girlfriend' website[8] for a quickie relationship. Or we might go for a one-night stand, or have a few 'friends with benefits'.

When relationships are messed up, the social institution that suffers the most is marriage. Over many decades, an increasing number of people haven't bothered to get married, but have opted to move in together instead. Over time, this has not only become socially acceptable, but normal. These days, in western society, living together is what people expect themselves, and everyone else, to do.[9] For those who bother

8   <http://www.dailylife.com.au/news-and-views/dl-opinion/do-men-really-prefer-rental-girlfriends-20130201-2dpy9.html>.
9   Andrews, K 2012, 'Soul mates and cohabitation' in *Maybe I Do: Modern Marriage & The Pursuit of Happiness*, Conner Court Publishing, Australia, pp. 191–218.

to get married, infidelity has become normal. Having an affair is no longer an act of treachery. It's just a way to have fun, a solution to getting bored with your regular partner.[10]

It is interesting that one-third of men who pay for sex also want to have a personal relationship with their sex worker escorts.[11] We can't actually separate our craving for physical sexual pleasure from a craving for a meaningful relationship with our sexual partner. Our body, our feelings, even our preferences (what people used to refer to as our 'conscience') rebels against such a separation, and annoyingly nags us with God's original, created purposes.

This hunt for sexual pleasure has also caused an alarming rise in unhealthy and abusive sexual activity. Our desires may be perverted to paedophilic and paraphilic[12] behaviour. Child sexual abuse and sex tourism are not just third world concerns; they happen in developed nations too, like Australia. As sex therapists are painfully aware, even couples who call themselves Christians engage in pornography and fringe sexual behaviours such as BDSM[13] and fetishes.[14]

Further, not all of us are confident in our gender (whether we're male or female). People are intersex, transgendered,

---

10   Gannon, G 2012, 'Natural born cheaters?' The Sydney Morning Herald, August 7, viewed June 7 2013, <http://www.smh.com.au/lifestyle/life/natural-born-cheaters-20120807-23rmn.html>.
11   Milrod, C & Weitzer, R 2012, 'The intimacy prism: Emotion management among the clients of escorts', Men and Masculinities, 15, pp. 447–467.
12   Repetitive sexual fantasies, urges, or behaviours that interfere with either satisfactory sexual relations or everyday functioning.
13   Bondage, Discipline and Sado-Masochism: sexual pleasure from giving or receiving pain.
14   Intense sexually arousing fantasies, urges or behaviours, where an individual uses a non-living object—for example, a woman's high-heeled shoe or lingerie—in a sexual manner.

cross-dressers and transsexual. Sometimes we do not desire the other gender, and may be homosexually oriented instead.

Our sexual brokenness also plays out at a societal level. Even with the easy availability of condoms, casual and risky sexual encounters are fuelling a rapid rise in the levels of sexually transmitted disease, mostly in our youth.[15] Families are unstable, and an increasing number of children live in foster care and single-parent households.[16] Youth suicide rates, drug use and mental illness are increasing. All of this puts more and more pressure on government and non-government welfare resources.

Some of you reading this will know all about these behaviours, and the damage they do, because you've been there. Reading about them may have torn open old wounds and brought guilt and shame to the surface. Again, there is really no better solution than this: Jesus! When we trust in him, we really are 'born again'. The old has gone, the new has come (2 Corinthians 5:17). If you find yourself plagued by shameful, guilt-inducing memories, talk to a sensible, mature, trustworthy minister or church leader. Those of you who are church leaders: be ready to walk with your people through the sordid memories of their past, until they reach the solid ground of confident trust in Christ again. As Paul writes, 'Carry each other's burdens, and in this way you will fulfil the law of Christ' (Galatians 6:2).

---

15   Middleton, M & McDonald, A 2013, 'Sexually transmissible infections among young people in Australia: An overview', *HIV Australia*, vol. 11, No. 1, March, pp. 9–10.
16   Parkinson, P 2011, 'For Kids' Sake. A Special Report on Repairing the Social Environment for Australian Children and Young People', viewed June 9 2013, <http://sydney.edu.au/law/news/docs_pdfs_images/2011/Sep/FKS-ResearchReport-Summary.pdf>.

Many of us have not behaved in such extreme sexual ways. Our personal sexual history may be much more conservative, so our memories may be quite healthy and happy. First of all, praise God! But be aware of the sexual failings that you do suffer from, even if they don't seem as degenerate as those of other people. Maybe it's lustful fantasy, temptation to use pornography or compulsive masturbation. Remember, 'we all stumble in many ways' (James 3:2a).

Remember the happy harmony between all the purposes of sexuality that we looked at in the previous chapter? The only way to achieve that harmony, in our sex lives and everything else, is to believe the Bible when it turns everything upside down. As people made new in Christ, God calls us to conform to his pattern for healthy sexuality. Let's have a look at what this lifestyle involves.

Restoring God's plan for sex

God is intensely interested in the purity of our sexual and relational life. Not only did Jesus limit sexual acts to marriage (Matthew 19:4–6), he even famously deemed sexual thoughts about a person you're not married to as being adulterous (Matthew 5:28), and included sexual immorality among the vices that demonstrate an impure heart (Mark 7:20–22). Paul made sexual behaviour a priority in living the holy life (1 Thessalonians 4:3–7).

Having been made new (born again) and completely forgiven in Christ, God calls us to:

... not conform to the pattern of this world, but be transformed by the renewing of your mind. Then you will be able to test and approve what God's will is—his good, pleasing and perfect will. (Romans 12:2)

As God's people, we are to live counterculturally. Whatever stage of life we are in—engaged, newlywed, parents, empty-nesters or in a retirement village—God calls us to conform to his pattern for sexuality and relationships. That means consciously rejecting the pattern of sexuality that everyone around us is following. This is going to be difficult, because every culture and society hates nonconformity. The Apostle Peter warned the Christians he was writing to that their former friends would 'heap abuse' on them for not joining in the flood of dissipation of 'debauchery, lust, drunkenness, orgies, carousing and detestable idolatry' (1 Peter 4:3–4). We will only be faithful to God's pattern if we are completely convinced that all of God's purposes for sexuality will work together (that happy harmony we noted earlier) to give us a lifetime of good sex. And that's why you need to keep reading this book—so you can see how it all works out.

God's basic pattern for sex is both simple and difficult. It's simple to understand, but very difficult to actually put into practice. That's the case with godliness, because it means going against both our old sinful self and the world's normal patterns, both of which are opposed to God.

Christian sexuality is 'cruciform'—it's patterned on the cross of Christ. We do this because it fulfils Jesus' summary of God's law: love God with your whole self, and 'love your neighbour as yourself' (Matthew 22:37–40; Mark 12:30–31;

Luke 10:27). Your spouse, who shares your bed, is the closest neighbour you're ever going to get. Let's be clear on this: to love others 'as yourself' doesn't mean you need to learn to love yourself before you can love others. That's just self-help therapy. Rather, it means to instinctively care for the other and protect them, just like you instinctively care for and protect yourself. So, to love your spouse 'as yourself' means to instinctively give life to, and protect, your spouse like you would yourself. And people, Christian or not, actually do that.

We now have a framework for understanding what God intends for us in our sex life. Having explored how society reflects the results of our rejection of God's plan, and having learned that we need to look to Christ for redemption, we are now ready to explore our bodies and relationships.

Part 2 describes the structure and function of the sexual parts of the bodies of males and females, while Part 3 is about making life choices in sexuality. We will explore what redeemed sexuality looks like at different stages of the life cycle, and contrast it with secular thinking and behaviour. Not surprisingly, there is congruence between the biological and social patterns of good sexuality, and God's model for sex and relationship. You will see that living God's way in your sex life as man and woman is a privilege. It is the only way to true, holistic, healthy relationships, and good sex.

Read on and be challenged to a countercultural lifestyle of healthy, pleasurable sex and intimate, satisfying relationships at every stage of your walk as a couple.

Take-away messages

- God gives us sex, as a gift and a blessing, for our good.
- God-honouring, Bible-patterned sexuality is good for us, as a couple, a family and a society.
- Marriage is God's place for the enjoyment and fulfilment of sexual intimacy.
- We see evidence of the need for redemption of sexuality and marriage in society and in the Church.
- No-one is beyond turning their life around and living their sex life as God designed it to be.

Part 2
Understanding your body as a sexual organ

All parts of our bodies, except for the parts involved in reproduction and sex, are similar in males and females. When it comes to these exceptions, we are created uniquely different, for the purpose of procreation—and recreation. This is a gift from God.

The Apostle Paul tells us that our body is a temple of the Lord, and not to be used for sexual immorality (1 Corinthians 6:18–20). This means our genitals, created with their special complementary structure and functions, are meant to be used in the appropriate one-flesh relationship of marriage (1 Corinthians 7:3–5).

This part of the book will help you understand what your genitals, and those of your spouse, look like and the changes that happen in them when you are sexually aroused. It is essential reading for engaged couples and newlyweds. However, we highly recommend it for all marrieds, whatever your age.

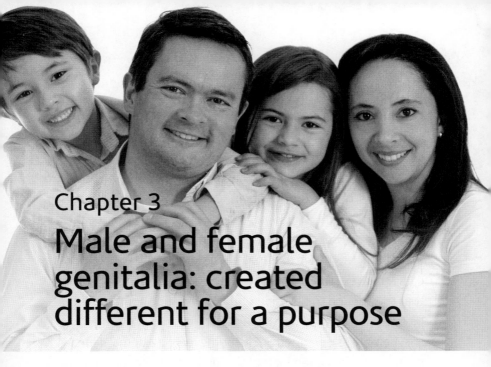

Chapter 3
Male and female genitalia: created different for a purpose

Whatever stage of relationship you are in, ignorance of what your body has to offer is not helpful in setting a basis for shared sexual intimacy. In this chapter, we will explore how your external genitalia, as man and woman, are perfectly complementary in structure and function.

You may think you know all about it. I recommend that you continue reading even if you think you do. When it comes to genitals and the sexual response, as a sex therapist, I am amazed at how ignorant many men and women are, even in this age of information overload. You may learn something new and exciting about your body or that of your spouse. You may be surprised at what this opens up in your lovemaking!

Female external genitalia (Sexualia)

For many, the female genitalia are a mystery beyond comprehension. So let's start there.

There are two parts to the female genitalia. Firstly, there are the internal reproductive parts: the vagina, leading to the uterus and out to the fallopian (uterine) tubes and the egg-producing ova. Most people, thanks to school sex education, have some comprehension of the structure and function of these. But the other external genitalia or, as we sexologists call it, the sexualia, remain a mystery. This is in spite of the fact that they are on the outside of the body, and should therefore be much easier to know and understand.

There are reasons for this. Firstly, the female external genitalia, hiding snugly between folds of skin under a hair-covered mound, are not as prominent as those of the male. So it's easy to ignore this part of the female body, or even pretend it doesn't exist.

Secondly, many girls are socialised to be ashamed of, rather than accept, their external genitals as a special part of their body. Little girls learn early that it's not nice to inquire or talk about, much less touch, these parts of their body. Words to describe the female external genitalia include euphemistic names like 'down there', 'front-bottom', 'privates' or even something absolutely meaningless like 'hoo-hoo'. As they grow, well-meaning parents, teachers and society in general tell girls that they have a 'vagina'. What girls need to hear is that they have a 'vulva'. The word vulva refers to the entire external genital area of the female. The vagina is the baby passage and penis-receiver in intercourse. Maybe adults don't say the word 'vulva' because it has connotations of sexual pleasure, and this makes them uncomfortable. Another word that is used to describe the vulva is 'crotch'. Apart from being a gender-neutral term, the word 'crotch' has nothing of the sensual feel that the word 'vulva' has when it is said.

As they grow and enter puberty, girls are given mixed messages about their body and genitalia. On one hand, in school sex education programs they learn about the reproductive system. Hormone changes, menstruation, pregnancy and contraception take centre stage; the uterus and vagina are discussed as the focus and source of these outcomes. The external genitalia and their role in sexual activity are rarely, if ever, discussed. If they are, it's about hygiene during menstruation, contraception and prevention of sexually transmitted infections.

In the playground and with their peer group, the message is very different. Music videos, internet, erotic literature, social media and pornography teach girls that the sexual parts of the body are to be exhibited and used to attract men. In a phenomenon called 'raunch culture', teenage girls flaunt their sexuality as a tool of power. The words they hear used for female genitalia are usually slang words used to denigrate[17], and often represent it as something to be used for male pleasure[18], with some even hinting at abuse.[19] This is not a constructive background for the development of healthy value systems and sexual self-esteem.

Unfortunately many parents, due to personal embarrassment and a mistaken opinion that schools provide all the sex education

---

17   The word 'clit' as a shortened form for clitoris, and others like 'cunt', 'fanny', 'gash', 'pussy', 'snatch' and 'twat' are used to insult someone or something as in 'You are such a clit' or 'It was such a gash'.
18   For example, words like 'cock-pocket', 'fish-taco', 'hot-pocket', 'pink canoe'.
19   For example, 'Axe-wound'.

needed, clam up on the topic of sex and sexuality. At a time when the developing teen brain is avidly integrating information into the neuronal circuits[20], parents and other adults fail to share their value systems and don't model healthy sexual and relational behaviour. This misinformation about what normal female genitalia look like continues into later life, with popular magazines and pornography propagating unrealistic and often unattainable images.

So, if you or your spouse feel ignorant about the female genitalia, don't worry—so are the majority of men and women around you!

Having an appreciation for the female genitalia is important for a satisfying sex life, irrespective of where you are in your journey as a couple. Just as important is an understanding of their structure and function. Every sex therapist has stories of couples who have been married five, ten or maybe 20 years or more, and have never looked at or talked about what lies in the mysterious area of the female external genitalia, much less the part it plays in their sexual activity. Their intimacy is a sort of dive for the pelvis or 'wham bam thank you ma'am' type of sexual activity.

The Bible tells us that our bodies as a whole, including the sex bits, are an integral part of the created goodness (Genesis 2:23–25). This means that the external genitalia are there for a purpose: for procreation (Genesis 1:28)—but also for the wonderful mutual pleasuring that establishes the one-flesh bonding of sex.

20   Weerakoon, P 2012, *Teen Sex By the Book*, Fervr, Sydney, pp. 50–51.

The Apostle Paul tells us that the whole body is meant to be shared in mutual, other-focused pleasuring and fun sexual activity within marriage:

> The wife does not have authority over her own body but yields it to her husband. In the same way, the husband does not have authority over his own body but yields it to his wife. (1 Corinthians 7:4)

And in the Song of Songs, the married couple enjoy each other's bodies. Here the allusions to the female external genitalia are couched in mutual love and the imagery of abundance, fertility, flowers and incense:

> My beloved is mine and I am his; he browses among the lilies. (2:16)

> Until the day breaks and the shadows flee, I will go to the mountain of myrrh and to the hill of incense. (4:6)

Read this as a couple; translate it to a language of your culture and location. Can you see the lover, the husband, browsing among the lilies? Enjoying all night the mountain of myrrh and hill of incense? How much more erotic and sexually positive can you get?

In this very eroticism lies the difference between God's view and the world's. The Bible portrays the female genitalia as something beautiful to be shared and enjoyed in other-focused sexual activity between a man and woman in marriage.

How does this compare with what the world portrays? Look around you at the internet, television, social media and especially pornography. How do you see the female genitalia portrayed? You will see an image far removed from what God

MALE AND FEMALE GENITALIA: CREATED DIFFERENT FOR A PURPOSE

45

meant it to be. The female genitals are portrayed as an object to be used (and often abused) for pleasure. They are used to gain self-gratification with the biggest orgasm, or as a tool to negotiate a sexual power over males. To this end females beautify, bleach and have a Brazilian[21] done; they even surgically enhance[22] or reduce their genitals to look like a *Playboy* centrefold or porn star. The surgical procedures in female genital cosmetic surgery are so popular that governments are considering public funding for these operations.[23]

Where does this leave a normal, healthy couple who want to enjoy sex as God intended?

For a woman it means knowing and loving the vulva you've got, and trusting your husband so much that you can share your body with him in no-shame sex. For the man, it's about learning the mysteries of your wife's body, recognising that it is a gift that she gives you, and that it is in God's plan that you pleasure her and nurture her, both emotionally and physically, when you are married.

So let's get to know the female external genitalia. Let's start with an exercise. Do this alone, and then discuss it with your partner. Look at diagram 1 on page 47. How many of the parts of the female genitalia can you name? Remember, this is a

---

21 The Brazilian wax is an extreme bikini-waxing treatment that removes hair from the entire pubic region, sometimes keeping a small patch just above the vaginal area, commonly dubbed the 'landing strip'.
22 Labiaplasty is surgery to reduce or reshape the labia major or labia minor of the female vulva. Vaginal reconstruction is supposed to tighten the passage to increase 'feeling'.
23 Hernandez, V 2013 'Aussie Government studying possibility of public funding for female private parts surgery', *International Business Times*, June 14, accessed June 16 2013, <http://au.ibtimes.com/articles/478562/20130614/aussie-government-studying-possibility-of-public-funding-female.htm#.UbpuE_nviSo>.

diagram; in real life every vulva is uniquely different in shape, size, colour, and even smell. No two women have identical vulvas. Even more importantly, there is no 'perfect' vulva. The drive for the smooth, hairless pubic area with hidden labia minor as the epitome of beauty is driven by the media and pornography. It is unrealistic and mostly unachievable.

In the diagram, the female has her legs separated to show the genital area or vulva. This includes her mons veneris (the mons), labia and the area between the labia called the vestibule, the urethral and vaginal openings, and the clitoris. The part behind the vulva and between that and the anus is called the perineum.

Diagram 1

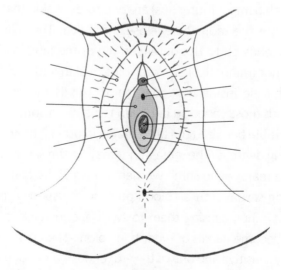

Now compare it with the labelled diagram in Appendix 1.

How many did you get right? What about your husband or fiancé?

Naming parts on a diagram is one thing, but seeing them in reality is another. If you are a woman, the next step is to identify these parts of the external genitalia *on your own body*. This is a useful exercise for you to do whatever your age or stage of life.

Get into bed after a nice hot shower or bath. Draw your feet up with your knees bent. Use a hand mirror and have a look at your own body. This is what you will find.

The mons veneris (mons) is the pad of soft fatty area that covers the pubic bone. It is covered by growth of hair after the onset of puberty. Hair removal by shaving, plucking, waxing, chemical depilation or laser treatment can cause problems such as inflammation or infection of the hair follicles or, in the case of laser treatment, darkening of the skin. So be careful if you choose to do these.

The labia major (outer lips) are two folds of skin that extend down from the mons to enclose the vulva. The hair on the mons extends on to the outer surface of the labia major. The labia minor (minor lips) are two folds of skin with soft spongy tissue that lie inside the labia major. This is the part of the vulva with most variation between females. In some, they are hardly visible between the labia major. In others, they protrude to varying degrees. The labia minor may be the same colour as the labia major or, in some women, they may be darker.

During sexual arousal, blood pools in the spongy tissues of the labia minor, causing them to swell and increase in size, as well as become darker or reddish in colour. The labia minor are also very sensitive and one of the erogenous[24] areas of the vulva.

---

24   The word 'erogenous' means sensitive to sexual stimulation.

Female genital cosmetic surgery (FGCS)

Whatever your vulva looks like, be assured—it is perfectly normal. Some females have genital cosmetic surgery (vaginal reconstruction, vulvoplasty, labiaplasty) to reduce and reshape the size of their labia minor or tighten the vaginal opening. A recent study[25] reports that the mean age of females undergoing surgery was 23 years, with some of those referred as young as 11 years. They report that, pre-operation, all those undergoing surgery would be considered within a normal range of labia minor size. They attribute this demand for surgery to the media, the internet and pornographic images of genitals.

The two sides of the labia minor meet at the front to form a hood over the clitoris. At the back, they meet behind the opening of the vagina. The area between them is called the vestibule. In this area are three things: the clitoris under the labial hood, the urethral opening and vaginal opening. Two glands called the Bartholin's glands, which secrete a thin watery fluid to keep the vulva moist, also open into the vestibule.

Let's look at the clitoris. What you see or feel of the clitoris is only the tip of a fascinating female organ. The little pearl-shaped structure (which, like the pearl, can vary greatly in size) nestled under the clitoral hood is called the glans of the clitoris. The glans of the clitoris is exquisitely sensitive. Most

25 Crouch, N, Deans, R, Michala, L, Liao, LM, & Creighton, S 2011, 'Clinical characteristics of well women seeking labial reduction surgery: a prospective study', *British Journal of Obstetrics and Gynaecology*, 118, pp. 1507–1510.

women are sexually aroused when it is touched gently (gently being the key word here). The very sensitivity of the glans means that harsh touch can be painful and can turn a woman off sex. The clitoris is in fact the only organ in the body whose sole purpose is to give pleasure. It does nothing else.

The glans curves up into the body of the clitoris. This is nestled under the skin, but can be felt. It separates into two cylinders of spongy erectile tissue that lie under the labia minor and attach to the bones of the pubis. These are called the crus and vestibular bulbs and have a structure similar to the erectile tissue of the penis.[26] They fill with blood when the woman is sexually aroused, forming a firm cushion around the urethra and vaginal opening, in readiness for the entry of the penis with maximum comfort and minimal trauma. This, together with Bartholin's gland secretions and the slippery fluid that escapes from the vagina when a woman is sexually aroused, makes the act of sexual intercourse comfortable and pleasurable. This is partly why sexual arousal is an important pre-event for satisfying sex in the woman.

Just behind the glans is the urethral opening for the passage of urine, and behind this the vaginal opening. The vaginal opening, or introitus, lies at the back part of the vestibule. In newborn girls, the vaginal introitus is covered by an incomplete fold of skin called the hymen. This flexible membrane has one, or several, holes to allow menstrual fluid to leave the body. It stretches as the girl is active, and if she uses tampons. No two girls have identical hymens. Depending on how small or large

---

26   O'Connell, HE, Sanjeevan, KV & Hutson, JM 2005, 'Anatomy of the clitoris', *The Journal of Urology*, 174, issue 4, part 1, pp. 1189–1195.

the opening is and how much of the hymen tissue is left, a girl may have some discomfort, even pain, on first intercourse. She may even bleed a little. However, this bleeding with first penetration happens in 50% or less of women. Rarely, a girl may have a thick hymen, and may need a minor surgical procedure called hymenectomy[27] before sexual intercourse is possible.

Virginity

The fact that (some) females bleed at first intercourse has resulted in the notion that the state of a female's hymen indicates whether she is a virgin. In some cultures it is still customary for the bride's mother or, even more embarrassingly, mother-in-law to display the blood-stained sheet as proof of the consummation of the marriage and the virginity of the bride. In some countries, females undergo hymen reconstruction surgery so that they can 'prove' their virginity.[28]

Looking beyond the vulva

The vulva is the portal to the reproductive system. And whereas it is not the intention of this chapter to discuss reproduction, the vagina leading into the pelvis (as the recipient of the penis in sexual intercourse) begs inclusion.

27 A minor medical procedure involving the surgical removal or opening of the hymen.
28 van Moorst, BR, van Lunsen, RHW, van Dijken, DKE & Salvator, CM 2012, 'Backgrounds of women applying for hymen reconstruction, the effects of counselling on myths and misunderstandings about virginity, and the results of hymen reconstruction', *The European Journal of Contraception and Reproductive Health Care*, 17, 2, pp. 93–105.

In some ways, the vagina is less of a mystery than the vulva. Girls are introduced to it at puberty as the conduit of menstrual flow and the location for tampons and sanitary products. Sex education classes teach both boys and girls the mechanics of sex, contraception and sexually transmitted diseases, generally all focusing on the vagina of a girl.

The vagina in an adult female is a collapsed tube about 8–10 cm long. It has a lining called the mucosa, which is surrounded by muscle and elastic tissue. It starts at the vulva and reaches up into the pelvis to the neck of the uterus (womb) at the cervix.

Some interesting points about the vagina:

- The vagina is incredibly adaptable and elastic. It can fit snugly around the thinnest penis. Think about it: it holds a tampon in place and yet can stretch to allow the passage of a baby's head!

- The lower (outer) third of the vagina is tighter and has more muscles and nerve endings. Thus most of the sensation (for both partners) comes from contact between the penis and this part.

- The lining of the vagina produces a secretion. This is normal and is part of the protective mechanism. It has a slightly musky odour. There is no need for douching or washing out the vagina. In fact, doing this could upset the chemical balance of the lining and cause irritation and infections.

When sexually aroused, the vaginal lining is suffused with blood. There is an increase in the fluid secretion, enough to be felt by the woman. It may even be so much as to wet the sheets. The aroused vagina also stiffens and opens up, lifting to a more vertical position. It is now ready for entry of the penis.

The 'G' or Grafenberg spot

This is probably one of the most controversial and elusive features of the vagina. It is said to be a spot about a third of the way into the front wall of the vagina, which when stimulated directly with the penis or a finger sends a female's arousal sky high. Does it exist? If it does, how come anatomists haven't located it?[29] Some females do report that they have such a spot, and some say not. Some also say that stimulation causes a spurt of fluid through the urethra. This has been interpreted as a 'female ejaculate'. None of this has any scientific proof. The fluid 'ejaculate' is more likely to be the secretion of what are called the paraurethral glands, resulting from the increased sensation and the pressure on the deep tissues of the clitoris.

Making love and arousing a woman is much more than a treasure hunt for the G spot. It is all-encompassing sexual activity that involves the brain and psyche as well as the body. It is as the Bible tells us: a beautiful, mutual and other-focused sharing of the body. For a woman, it is a relationship in which she can share the most intimate parts of her body with her husband, knowing that he will not laugh at or degrade her in any way. We see this expressed in the whole of the Song of Songs.

The big 'O' for females

What is the female orgasm?

---

29   Kilchevsky, A, Vardi, Y, Lowenstein, L & Gruenwald, I 2012, 'Is the Female G-Spot Truly a Distinct Anatomic Entity?', *Journal of Sexual Medicine*, No. 9, pp. 719–726.

There are some similarities in the female and male orgasm. In both, it is a feeling of intense pleasure followed by release and calmness. This release is appropriately given the title 'climax'. There is a brief, somewhat rhythmic contraction of the genital area that often spreads to a generalised tension of muscles in the rest of the body. Respiratory rate, heart rate and blood pressure go up, sometimes causing deep and gasping breathing and a visible reddish flush over the skin. Pupils dilate and the approaching climax may even cause vocalisation and involuntary groans.

In the brain, an orgasm causes a spike of the hormone oxytocin and other pleasure chemicals such as endorphins. These result in a feeling of euphoria and sometimes even a fleeting feeling of loss of conscious thought. This has earned orgasm the name 'la petite mort' or the small death.

There are, however, differences between the orgasms of men and women. In the man, the orgasm is accompanied by an ejaculation of seminal fluid from the penis. In the woman, the only consistent feature is the rhythmic contraction of the muscles around the lower vagina (muscles that form what is called the pelvic floor, mainly the pubococcygeus). It is much more subtle than in the man—and elusive. Some say this is an intrinsic part of the 'feminine mystique'. Further, orgasms are tremendously variable between women, and interestingly, even between sexual experiences in an individual. Further, the orgasmic feelings of vaginal intercourse may vary dramatically from that of oral sex, or direct stimulation of the clitoris and genitalia. Researchers tell us that a third to 50% of women never have orgasms during sexual intercourse[30], although most of these can orgasm with clitoral or other genital stimulation. And although there are women who have multiple orgasmic experiences during one sexual encounter, this is the exception rather than the norm.

Importantly, sexual satisfaction in women is not directly related to the strength of muscle contractions or brain sensations in orgasms. Many women, who by clinical standards do not have an orgasm with sexual activity, tell us that they are satisfied and enjoy the experience very much. For them, orgasms are nice but not necessary for sexual pleasure. Another point is that an orgasm is *not* a requirement for a woman to get pregnant.

If you are a woman, you now know what your genitalia look like, and if you did examine yourself, you also know how they feel. If you are reading this in your engagement period, it is advisable to visit your general practitioner and get a medical examination done before the wedding. This will give you an opening to discuss contraception if you plan to use it, and is best done a couple of months before the wedding.

If you are a man and engaged to be married, you now have an idea—something like a road map—of the genital region of your fiancée. You can approach your honeymoon lovemaking with a little more confidence. If you are a married man, your wife will be pleased that you have a better understanding of her body. She may even be happy for a 'show and tell' or reintroduction! Work this into your lovemaking.

30   Wallen, K & Lloyd, EA 2011, 'Female sexual arousal: Genital anatomy and orgasm in intercourse', *Hormones and Behavior*, 59, 5, pp. 780–792.

The section that follows is advice to girls who are engaged to be married. It's about getting your genitalia ready for sexual activity. It is an activity that is *useful but not essential*. Some of you may not be comfortable doing this. And that is OK.

For those women reading this who are already married and have had sex, the exercise will help you feel more comfortable and confident with your vulva. If you have discomfort during intercourse, it will help you to relax.

Let me say up-front that these activities are not masturbation. Masturbation is solo self-stimulation for the precise purpose of sexual arousal and pleasure. The exercises below are to prepare your body for the other-focused lovemaking you will enjoy in marriage.

Vaginal introitus massage

The opening of the vagina and the immediate area around it is called the introitus (entry). The skin in this area is sensitive, especially at the back. The exercise below will prepare this area for the entry of the penis in sexual intercourse.

As before, have a nice hot shower or a bath with some relaxing bath oil. Get into bed and draw your feet up with the knees bent. Dip your fingers in some baby oil or mild water-based lubricant. Trace the edge of your vaginal opening with your fingers. Concentrate your attentions on what you are feeling. Be mindful of the sensations. It may be uncomfortable at the beginning. Or it may feel tingly and nice. Either way, stay with the feelings. Consciously relax the muscles of your thighs and your pelvis. Do this a couple of times. Now move two fingers to the back of the vaginal opening and press down firmly. You should feel a deep pressure.

If you are comfortable doing it, insert one and then two fingers into your vagina. When you have two fingers in, gently stretch the vaginal opening by moving your fingers apart.

Do this exercise for a few minutes every night. Your vagina will now be better prepared for the sensations that accompany the penis pushing at the introitus.

Pelvic muscle exercises

These exercises work the pubococcygeus (PC) muscle. We have already come across this as the pelvic floor muscle that contracts during orgasm. Exercising it will enable you to relax the muscles around the vagina during lovemaking. This will give the penis easier access, and lessen any discomfort you feel. A side effect will be that you are likely to have better orgasmic contractions.

Firstly, identify the PC muscle. Pretend that you are urinating, and then try to stop the flow with a quick muscle contraction. That muscle you just used to stop the flow from the bladder is your PC muscle. Try to keep your stomach and thigh muscles relaxed and focus only on the PC muscle.

Now exercise it. Contract the PC muscle 20 times. Hold it for one or two seconds each time, then release. Be mindful of the sensations as you contract and as you relax. Repeat this three times a day, three to four times per week. Breathe normally during this exercise and try to avoid holding your breath. Once you become used to this exercise, you will find that you can do them at any time. In the car when stuck at a traffic light, while you're on the phone—anywhere.

We now move on to the male.

Male external genitalia

As with females, there are both internal genitalia (hidden) and external parts (visible) of the male body. The difference is that, unlike the vulva, the external genitalia in the male are mostly all 'out there'.

The penis is the male body part least exposed in public, and yet for many men, it is the very centre of masculinity and body image. Even the word used for failing to achieve an erection—impotency—links the penis with masculine power or its absence. Slang words like 'purple-headed warrior', 'anaconda', 'manhood' and even 'battering ram' bring images of the penis as a symbol of male authority and potency.

If you are an engaged couple, you are preparing to enter this wonderful intimate union of marriage. Just as you learned about the woman, you now need to understand how the penis works. If you are already married and think you know all about your genitals (or your husband's), please read on anyway. Who knows? You may learn something that enhances your love-life!

In this section, we will consider some common penis questions like, what does a normal penis look like? Is mine (or my partner's) too small? Thin? Long? Short? Curved?

There are other questions you may have, like the many ways the penis can be used in lovemaking, and what to do when it doesn't work to plan. We will discuss these questions and possible problems later in the book.

What is normal? And what makes it behave the way it does?
The penis comes in shades of pink, brown and black. Every single one is different. And yet, each is an independent engineering marvel like no other part of the body.

Surprisingly, many men don't know what their penis looks like, much less the range carried by others. They may have a quick peek at their neighbour's at the urinals or in the change rooms. That's about the extent of their education. Sadly, for many men today, the expectation of a normal penis is built on the unrealistic portrayals of male genitalia in pornography.

Women learn about the penis from friends and magazines, and more recently from pornography, both visual and written. For many women the first sight of an erect penis is either a disappointment or a shock.

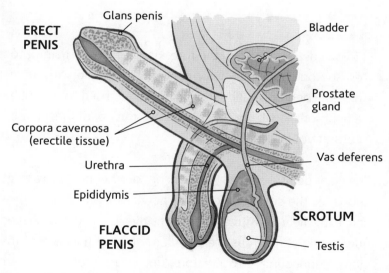

ERECT PENIS

Glans penis

Bladder

Corpora cavernosa (erectile tissue)

Prostate gland

Urethra

Vas deferens

Epididymis

SCROTUM

FLACCID PENIS

Testis

The penis has a body or shaft and a slightly bulbous tip called the glans penis. If you are fair-skinned, you may see a thick bluish line on the upper or dorsal surface of the penis. This is caused by a blood vessel, the dorsal vein, and is perfectly normal. The skin over the penis is loose and elastic and extends over the glans penis to form the prepuce or foreskin. If you have been circumcised you will not have this fold of skin.

At the tip of the glans is a slit-like opening. This is called the urethral meatus. This is where both urine and semen come out, but not at the same time. A valve at the base of the urethral (urine) tube makes sure that only urine comes out when you urinate and semen when you ejaculate.

In an uncircumcised penis, the foreskin should glide back easily over the glans. As a boy you should have learned to pull the foreskin back and clean your glans penis when you bathe. It is important to do this. Secretions known as smegma collect under the foreskin and can cause infections, some say even cancer.

Alert

If you cannot pull back the foreskin, or else it is painful to do so you should see your general practitioner. You may have a condition called Phimosis, a word used to describe a tight foreskin. If you think you have this condition, please consult your doctor.

The glans penis is shaped like an acorn or a helmet with a ridge known as the corona or crown. The glans is smooth, hairless and extremely sensitive. Most sensitive is a little Y-shaped ridge of skin known as the frenulum on the underside of the glans, connecting it to the foreskin. In uncircumcised men, the glans is covered with pink, moist skin called mucosa. In circumcised men, the foreskin is surgically removed and the mucosa on the glans transforms into dry skin.

During sexual activity (sexual intercourse, masturbation or oral sex), friction of the foreskin over the frenulum and glans, or if you are circumcised, direct stimulation on the glans is very sexually arousing. This is a truly erogenous zone for a man.

Behind the penis is a loose sac of skin, the scrotum. Called by the slang words of 'balls', 'nut sack' and 'coin sack' among many other terms, this contains the sperm-producing organs, the pair of testes. The testes lie side by side in the scrotum, separated by a central septum of tissue.

Now you know what the male genitalia look like. But if you are a man, you may have a niggling worry. How do I compare with others? Am I too small? Can I satisfy my wife?

You're not alone in worrying about your penis size and function. Society tells us that he who has the most wins. Since bigger is better, the capacity to be a good lover must be possible only with a large penis. So, many men aspire to and admire the gladiator image of the fantasy penis seen in pornography: an erection to match the Taj Mahal that lasts as long as the Himalayas.

No amount of explanation on genetic and cultural variations of penis size, or the fact that penis size is irrelevant to most women when rating a lover as good or bad, can convince some men that size doesn't matter. Nor do men understand that what you see is not what you've got. A larger pubic fat pad or abdominal obesity would result in only a small part of the penis being visible externally—kind of like looking at the tip of the iceberg.

In general, the average penile length is 9.0–9.5 cm in the flaccid (non-erect) state.[31] Average erect penile length ranges from 12.8–14.5 cm and erect penile girth is 10.0–10.5 cm. Remember this is an average. Actual lengths vary greatly. If you fall short of the flaccid norm in size, take heart: the small starters gain proportionally more on erection.

---

31   Dillon BE, Chama, NB & Honig, SC 2008, 'Penile size and penile enlargement surgery: a review', *International Journal of Impotence Research*, 20, pp. 519–529.

It is also a fact that most women, while appreciating a penis of average length and an erect width to fit and stimulate the vagina, are more interested in the attention a man gives them—the foreplay and romance. In a study, 20% of females interviewed agreed that the length of the penis was 'at all important' and only 1% deemed it 'very important'.[32]

Every therapist has a story of a male with a perfectly normal penis pleading and then demanding to be given a drug to enhance his organ, ignoring advice on lifestyle and nutrition but insisting on a referral for penis enhancement.

As Christians, we know that we are not defined by our bank account, the suburb we live in, the car we drive, or our body size, shape or colour—and definitely not by our genital size or shape, or our sexual prowess. We're defined by God's love for us, demonstrated and enacted in Christ Jesus (1 John 3:1). So stop worrying and enjoy what God has given you by using it as he has patterned it to be used.

Let me finish with a special word of warning. The desire for a bigger and better penis is met by procedures and devices claiming to enhance penile size, and widely advertised on the internet. Suction devices, penis extension frames and assorted medications and patches are widely promoted. Take care. Here it is very much 'caveat emptor': buyer beware. Some of these untested and expensive techniques promise results so ambitious as to be comical. There is no evidence in the literature that these procedures have a long-term effect on the

---

32   Francken, AB, van de Wiel, HB, van Driel, MF & Weijmar Schultz, WC 2002, 'What importance do women attribute to the size of the penis?', *European Urology*, 42, pp. 426–431.

increase of penis length or width. They could lead to deformity and erectile dysfunction.

Currently, there is little consensus in the medical community over the indications for penile augmentation surgery. Globally, most medical, surgical and urological associations recommend counselling, psychotherapy and education rather than cosmetic penile surgery for men with normal penises who want enhancement.[33]

My advice is: do not even consider these.

What happens in the penis when a man is sexually aroused?

The penis has an intricate plumbing network of blood vessels. The inside of the penis is made up of three columns of spongy tissue. The paired corpora cavernosa lie on either side of the single corpus spongiosum which carries the urethra and ends in the glans penis. In a flaccid (non-erect) penis, the spaces in the sponge have just a trickle of blood flowing in and out of them. The walls of the spaces are lined with a type of muscle called smooth muscle. This muscle is different to that in the arms or legs. The muscles lining the spongy spaces respond to sexual arousal by relaxing. They can't be willed into action like the muscles of your arms and legs. The columns of spongy tissue are surrounded by a thin fibrous sheath called the tunica albuginea. This sheath is about the thickness of a page in a glossy magazine, and as resistant to stretch.

When a man is sexually aroused, a frisson of sexual excitement starts in the brain and races down the spinal cord.

33   Wylie, KR & Eardley, I 2007, 'Penile size and the "small penis syndrome"', *British Journal of Urology International*, 99, pp. 1449–1455.

Nerves at the lower end of the spinal cord send out 'whoopee' signals to the penis. What happens next is what causes the penis to firm and enlarge.

Blood vessels to the penis open up and blood shoots in. Now, the smooth muscles that line the walls of the spongy spaces in the corpora cavernosa and corpus spongiosum relax. The spaces are now open. Blood flows into these spaces. As the spongy spaces fill up, the blood outflow vessels, the veins (channels taking blood away from the penis) which go through the fibrous tunica albuginea get pressed and finally close.

Follow what's happening? There's more blood coming in than going out. And it happens—an enlarged and tumescent penis. This is an erection.

Wait a minute. How come it doesn't grow … and grow… and … you know what I mean. That's because of the firm sheath of tissue, the tunica albuginea. It determines the size and rigidity of the penis. Further, the corpora cavernosa separate out at the base to attach to the bones of your pelvis (on what is called the ischiopubic rami), keeping the erect penis firmly attached and not floundering around aimlessly.

What about the third column of spongy tissue: the corpus spongiosum? This has no firm sheath of fibrous tissue. However its filling is limited by the fact that it nestles between the two firm corpora cavernosa. It stays firm but not rigid, keeping the urethral sperm carrier tube open. All is now ready for action.

The big 'O' for men

In a man, the orgasm is the end point of a sexual arousal experience. That's why it's called a 'climax'. There are actually two parts to this experience. One is the cosmic explosion of exhilaration that takes place in the brain, driven by a cocktail of pleasure and satiety chemicals such as dopamine, oxytocin and endorphins. This is equivalent to the brain orgasm experienced by women. The second is the pelvic act of semen ('cum', ejaculate, 'juice') moving from its storage place in the tubes (epididymis) close to the testes in the scrotum to the outside through the vas deferens and urethra—a process known as ejaculation. For most men, these two parts happen simultaneously.

You now know what the male and female genitalia look like and how they function in sexual arousal. Recognise them both for what they are: a marvel of creation with the power to give exquisite pleasure while gaining complete personal contentment. Focus on using your genitals for other-focused pleasure and procreation, and truly delight in it.

We now move on to what happens when man and woman come together to make love.

Take-away messages

- The size and appearance of the external genitals vary between individuals.

- Your sexual function is not determined by the size or shape of your penis or vulva.

- As a Christian created as an image bearer of God, your identity lies in Christ, not in what your body or your sexual organs look like, or how they function.

Chapter 4
Male and female sexual response: different and complementary

In God's created order, the male and female bodies are made to respond to each other in a way that gives pleasure to both, while fulfilling the command to procreate.

Whatever the sexual activity, and whether it be for procreation, recreation or some other purpose such as stress relief, the body and brain respond in a particular manner. There is sexual desire, which is a brain event signalling a need or motivation for sex, the body response of sexual arousal, and finally, the brain recognition of this build-up of sexual tension resulting in orgasmic release.

First, a couple of general points about the sexual response.

Males and females are different in the way that sexual desire, arousal and orgasm are perceived and even sequenced in the sexual response. An ignorance of this difference in the sexual response between males and females is the most common cause of sexual concerns in married life.

There is also a plethora of individual variations in desire, arousal and orgasm—all within the normal range. No two individuals respond in exactly the same way, and a person's response will vary depending on the context of the sexual activity, their partner, and their stage in life. Further, the intensity of sexual desire and the specific 'turn on' factors will be influenced by everything that has been fed into the brain—the script we each carry.

With these in mind, let's look at the male and female sexual response.

The male sexual response

Although men vary considerably in their individual interest in sex, the average man does tend to be much more 'driven' sexually than the woman. As a relationship progresses, a man's sexual desire tends to remain high, whereas the woman's desire is found to decrease.

It is also true that men are more easily turned on than women by the 'senses'. By this we mean sight, smell and sound. A cleavage, a nice bottom, the whiff of a particular fragrance, the sound of heavy breathing, all act as quick and easy sexual turn-on stimuli for most men.

Once sexual desire sets in, an erection generally follows, and then the ejaculation. This linear pattern of sexual response (desire –> arousal –> orgasm –> resolution) is set early in development in the male. An adolescent male learns that when he is turned on, his sexual desire followed by erection and orgasm is both pleasurable and fun. This remains into adult life.

So, broadly speaking:

- Males are keener than females on the physical aspect of sex, especially genital activity.
- No matter how romantic and gentle a man may be, deep down one of his major objectives (learned from youth) is penile–vaginal intercourse.
- In intercourse, men strive for ejaculation and orgasm.
- Since the penis is so important to men, most enjoy other sexual activities that involve this organ such as oral sex and having their penis directly stimulated by the woman (sometimes called mutual masturbation).
- Since the genitals and the act of sexual intercourse are so important, a man may feel rejected and sad if the woman he loves refuses to engage in sexual activity with him.

We now move to the female. For the men reading this, I am sure it will come as no surprise to learn that in terms of the sexual response, women are more complex than you are.

The female sexual response

A woman's motivation for sexual activity is multifaceted. Sometimes it is a testosterone and neurochemical-driven, spontaneous appetite for sex, as in men. However, this is the rarity rather than the norm. Most often, the motivation to engage in sexual activity depends on what's happening at that moment—the immediate context. It is driven by a wish for intimacy, a commitment to the relationship, remembered feelings of closeness and satisfaction from prior sexual experiences with the partner, even an appreciation of what the partner is doing for her at the time. Maybe it is because she wants to get pregnant, and today's the day. Sometimes it is a sense of doing the right thing, a sense of offering her body as a gift for the sexual satisfaction of her husband. On the negative side, a female can use sex as a tool of power or manipulation, and even a job, as in sex work.

Whatever the motivation, what happens next in the woman is interesting. Unlike in the man, where sexual desire is necessary to drive the changes of genital arousal (an erection), in the woman the onset of sexual activity and the sensual touching, loving words and general romancing by her husband results in the physiological changes of arousal in the genitals. She will feel the vaginal swelling and wetting. It is after this that the woman begins to feel the brain changes of sexual desire. This 'responsive' sexual desire can then feed back to increase the body arousal levels. So, as she relaxes and allows herself to enjoy being made love to, her body and brain respond. And, unlike men, many females describe the outcome of sexual activity as physically rewarding, even 'satiating' without necessarily experiencing orgasm. This satisfaction feeds back to feelings of intimacy, completing a circle.

We end up with what is called 'a circular intimacy driven model'[34] of sexual response in females.

34   Basson, R 2000, 'The female sexual response: A different model', *Journal of Sex & Marital Therapy*, 26:1, pp. 51–65.

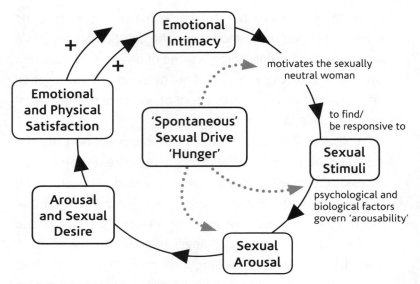

So, broadly speaking, in women:

- A feeling of sexual desire is not necessary to be able to consent to or start sexual activity. Rather, it is the context in which the lovemaking happens that is important.
- Unlike men, genital arousal can be felt before, and can stimulate, desire.
- Satisfying sexual activity is possible, even without an orgasm.

How should a couple enjoy the complementary sexual response?

As husband and wife, we should understand and work with the difference of the male and female sexual responses. Look at the marriage passage in Ephesians 5:22–28. Here Paul speaks of the husband leading, and the wife following in sweet surrender.

How can we apply this to sexual activity?

The husband is called to love his wife in the way Christ loves the Church: pursuing her even when she is unworthy, sacrificing his body even to the point of death for her good and her holiness. The husband is called to lead, spiritually and physically, and, sexually speaking, this would include romancing her in the home and in the bedroom. It's easier for the wife. She is called to allow him to arouse her, romance her and love her to distraction; to invite him into her sexuality. Women are like a slow-cooking crockpot to the man's quick heat-up microwave desire. Recognise it and enjoy it. These complementary roles of leadership and sweet submission don't come easy for some of us. And yet, this is exactly how the male and female sexual response is set up in the brain for most men and women.

But wait. There will be some women who are easily aroused, and who like to initiate sex. This too is just fine. Others may be neutral sometimes and allow their husband to drive their desire, and may be the initiators at other times. You can see this in the diagram of the female response (page 70). Likewise there are some men who do not fit into the male model of rapid-fire sexual arousal. They may take longer to develop sexual desire, and may prefer their spouse to be the initiator of sexual intimacy. This too is OK.

Whatever your pattern of arousal and response, discuss it, and weave your lovemaking around it. Enjoy what you have. Vive la différence!

Your times of lovemaking wax and wane though married life. Use your knowledge of the sexual response to your advantage. Don't stress on the performance; don't go searching for the missing libido (desire) or yearn for the simultaneous orgasm. Enjoy the fact that as man and woman, God created you different. As a married couple relive your love story. Bring back those dopamine-fuelled love moments on an occasional date night. Make time for intimacy. There is a biblical precedent for this in Deuteronomy 24:5. A man recently married was given a years' leave so he could be 'free to stay at home and bring happiness to the wife he has married'. You may not get a year's leave for an extended honeymoon of lovemaking. But you can carve out quality time for each other. Learn how best to synchronise your individual sexual response cycles. We will discuss this more in Part 3.

Take-away messages

- The male and female genitalia are created to function together as a pair in lovemaking.

- The sexual response in males and females provides a complementary function where the man can take the lead in romancing his wife.

- There is an individual variation. Learn your and your partner's sexual response, likes and dislikes, and weave these into your lovemaking.

Part 3
Sex and the life cycle

You are a sexual being from the moment you are born to the moment you die. You do not suddenly become sexual when you are a teenager, begin dating or get married. However, you become part of a couple when you move into a serious relationship with a person of the opposite sex. As a Christian couple, the time when you are engaged to be married is the point when a serious relationship is established. All that has gone before has been the time of searching and preparation for this special relationship. We will therefore start our journey of a lifetime of good sex at the engagement period.

Come with us as we trace the sexual story a couple builds from the time they are engaged to be married, through marriage, babies and, finally, to when they are in a retirement village or nursing home. We will discuss changes in the body and sexual function. At each stage, I will challenge you with candid snapshots of personal and couple scenarios, and invite you to consider the choices available through God's plan for the best sex—in marriage.

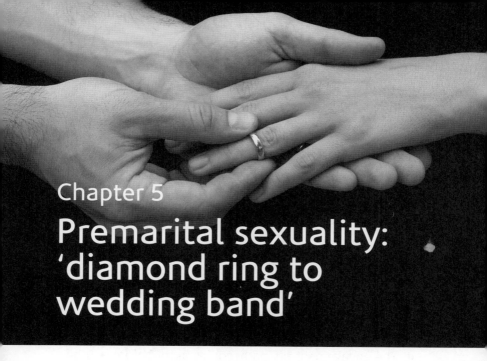

Chapter 5
Premarital sexuality: 'diamond ring to wedding band'

You're with your friends at the beach. It's a magical sunset on a clear summer's night. Someone turns on their CD player. Your friends are up singing and dancing. Others join in—it's a flash mob. And they start singing:

> 'It's a beautiful night, we're looking for something dumb to do
> Hey baby, I think I wanna marry you'.[35]

Your boyfriend drops down on one knee.

> 'Will you marry me?'

You don't know whether to laugh or cry.

> 'Yes ... yes ... yes.'

---

35   Bruno Mars, *Marry you*, Atlantic/Elektra, 2011. Referenced from <http://www.azlyrics.com/lyrics/brunomars/marryyou.html>.

Well, maybe your proposal wasn't quite like that. But you have the ring on your finger; you are now a couple.

What next? What does this time between the diamond ring and wedding band involve? Is it just a time for planning the wedding ceremony? How many bridesmaids should you have? Who will be groomsmen? There are many things to organise, such as the hall, the catering, the music and the perfect wedding gown ... and don't forget the church service.

Maybe it's a long engagement, in which you plan to save money for a car or a house, to make sure you start off with all the niceties of married life.

Or perhaps, as a couple, you decide that you need to check out whether you can really stand to be together day in and day out. The engagement period becomes a 'try before you buy' time; a sort of semi-commitment, a quasi-contract. You move in together and join the cohabitation couples' club.

And when it comes to sex, perhaps you feel it's time to come out of the closet. Maybe you have been sexually active as a couple, but have kept it a secret. Now you feel you can legitimately continue and be public about it. After all, everyone's doing it. And you are planning to get married soon.

Or maybe you have kept yourselves pure; all you've done is hold hands, or maybe kiss and cuddle. Now you wonder: does being engaged give you a licence to move into deeper levels of sexual intimacy? You know the Bible says sexual intimacy is to be reserved for marriage. But this seems impossible when you love your partner deeply, and when you're together daily for six months ... 12 months ... or even longer. The media, internet, advertisements—even your friends—tell you how wonderful sex is. Intercourse orgasms, they say, are mind-blowing. The range of activities is endless. It all sounds amazing, and you want to experiment, push the boundaries of physical intimacy.

Why wait?

The Bible and the engagement period

The Bible does not give us clear directions for male–female relationships in the engagement period. This is probably because, in biblical times, marriages were arranged by parents and there was no specific engagement period where a couple prepared for marriage. And premarital sex, called fornication, was taboo anyway.

There are, however, a few instances in the Bible where we encounter the circumstances of a man and woman 'pledged to be married'.

In the Old Testament we read of laws surrounding virgins and those pledged to be married. Exodus 22:16 refers to the social responsibility that follows sexual intercourse:

> *If a man seduces a virgin who is not pledged to be married and sleeps with her, he must pay the bride-price, and she shall be his wife.* (Exodus 22:16)

In biblical times, being 'pledged to be married' was seen as being legally married, but not yet in a sexually-consummated union. The sexual union was so important that men were to be sent home from battle to consummate the relationship (Deuteronomy 20:7).

The perfect example of behaviour in a couple pledged to be married comes from the New Testament. Yes, the story of Joseph and Mary. In Matthew 1:18–19 we read of Joseph's response to the news that his fiancée is pregnant—and clearly not by him.

> *This is how the birth of Jesus the Messiah came about: His mother Mary was pledged to be married to Joseph, but before they came together, she was found to be pregnant through the Holy Spirit. Because Joseph her husband was faithful to the law, and yet did not want to expose her to public disgrace, he had in mind to divorce her quietly.*

But once the angel explained God's plan to him, Joseph acted differently:

> *When Joseph woke up, he did what the angel of the Lord had commanded him and took Mary home as his wife. But he did not consummate their marriage until she gave birth to a son. And he gave him the name Jesus.* (Matthew 1:24–25)

Here we see a man who loved his betrothed deeply. He loved her even when he thought that she had been sexually unfaithful to him. He had the chance to protect himself, and expose Mary to public scorn, but he didn't. In this messy situation, he did what he could to protect her. Then, once Joseph knew God's plan for the unborn baby, he demonstrated total obedience and sexual self-control. Joseph was faithful—faithful to Mary and to God's commands. Think about it: this was the kind of reliable, caring, protecting character to whom God entrusted his only begotten Son. God the Father considered Joseph worthy, and trusted him in the role of earthly father, to nurture Jesus.

Here we learn broad biblical principles. But how do these work out in our times?

Let's go back to the question at the start of this chapter: 'Will you marry me?' The question asked by the man and the excited 'yes' from the woman implies an agreement. They make a promise to each other to use the engagement period to prepare themselves for the union of man and woman that marriage involves.

Do you, as a couple, understand what marriage truly means? Let's start by discussing what a Christian marriage is *not*.

It is *not* a contract that is nullified if either party doesn't keep to the prenuptial agreement, or where a partner moves on if he or she is dissatisfied sexually or otherwise. It is also not an open relationship where infidelity is accepted. It is not even a duty bond that keeps you bound as husband and wife, where faithfulness is a chore rather than a joy.

Christian marriage is a covenant relationship between a man and a woman, a one-flesh, naked and no-shame bond between them (Genesis 2:23–25). It is a lifelong union (Matthew 19:4–6); an exclusive, intimate connection between them which mirrors the exclusive, intimate relationship between Christ and the Church (Ephesians 5:21–33). In the Christian marriage ceremony, a person agrees to take their wife or husband to 'live together according to God's law. To give [the other] the honour due to [them] as [their] wife/husband and, forsaking all others, love and protect [the other] as long as [they] both shall live'.[36]

---

36   Marriage Form 1 (2012), *Common Prayer: Resources for Gospel-shaped Gatherings*, Anglican Press Australia, Sydney.

They vow 'to have and to hold from this day forward, for better for worse, for richer or poorer, in sickness and in health, to love and to cherish, as long as we both shall live'.[37] These are powerful declarations made before their family and friends in the presence of God.

Jesus spoke strongly on the permanence of marriage (Mark 10:11–12), as did Paul (1 Corinthians 7:10–13).

The Genesis 2 narrative of marriage uses the phrase 'united' for the marriage relationship. This means to stick or hold together and resist separation. The marriage proposal and its acceptance is the mutual promise of this cleaving together for life. The engagement period is one of preparation for this lifelong 'gluing' together as man and wife.

How do two people who come from two very different families, with different parenting and behaviour patterns, do this?

You need to build on the foundation of the proposal promise. This is going to feel unusual, because initially you'll be in the haze of romantic love where the other seems faultless and wonderful. So you need to be reminded that this person God has given you isn't all that perfect. Every person who marries is a sinner (that means both of you!) so neither searching for a spouse, nor preparing to be a spouse, is a pursuit of perfection. It's a decision to work together, as two flawed followers of Jesus, to build the foundations of a marriage that will mirror Christ's love.

The engagement period is a time when the engaged couple get to *know* each other. And this means spending time together in communication—talking.

37   ibid.

This time is a window of opportunity to learn about each other, to iron out those 'you do/want/expect what?' moments. You may think you are already doing this. After all, you spend hours together, your eyes locked saying 'I love you', 'you are the best thing that has happened to me', 'you are perfect', and the other sweet nothings that lovers share. This is not what I mean. Time needs to be taken for discussing values, attitudes and beliefs, and how these may impact the relationship you are to enter into. And sex is an important part of this—just not the whole.

This book is a book on sex, so we don't have the space to discuss this relational aspect of marriage preparation in detail. An excellent resource with which to do this is a short e-book by John Piper called *Preparing for Marriage*.[38] Take time to read it; discuss the questions. Understanding the sovereignty of God and his plan for your marriage will put sexual activity in its place. Sex is a wonderful and exciting gift from God to us. In your highly erotic state of waiting for marriage it may be difficult for you to accept that sex is *not* the most important thing in your marriage relationship. Keep reminding yourself, and each other, that it is just one part and not the whole.

You need to see the full picture of the marriage relationship to savour the sexual element in it. Your church may also offer marriage preparation courses such as *Prepare Enrich*.[39] Take the time to thoughtfully and prayerfully engage in this preparation. In marriage you are to be yoked together for life!

---

38   Free e-book, viewed on February 11 2013 at <http://www.desiringgod.org/resource-library/books/preparing-for-marriage>.
39   See <http://www.prepare-enrich.com.au/>.

Deuteronomy 22:10 tells us, 'Do not plough with an ox and a donkey yoked together'. Get your values and attitudes in sync before marriage. Take at least as much time to prepare spiritually and emotionally for marriage as you spend planning the wedding ceremony and the honeymoon. You are going to be ploughing together with the same yoke for a very long time.

Honest communication is not always easy. Past experiences, sexual and otherwise, will come up in your conversation. These can be painful for both of you. Maybe you have been sexually active, have watched pornography, or have been a habitual masturbator. Or perhaps you have been the victim of child sexual abuse or violence. In the covenant marriage relationship, you are committing to your future as a married couple. Whatever you did or desired sexually in the past is just that—in the past.

In Romans 8:1, Paul writes, 'There is now no condemnation for those who are in Christ Jesus'. Trust in the promise. Repent. Seek forgiveness from God and each other. Then leave the past in the past, and move forward together.

There is one proviso we need to add here. Some sexual sins, like childhood abuse and sexually inappropriate behaviours, leave deep scars. If you feel that this is your situation, then you need to seek help from an older, wiser Christian couple, your pastor or a counsellor. It may involve confession of past sexual and other sins. Remember, the body of Christ is there to help you. In James 5:16 we are advised to confess our sins to each other and pray for each other. Don't be ashamed or guilty. And don't put it off.

And one more piece of advice: talking about sex while not being sexually intimate is not easy. So, take it slow. Don't ramp up the language or discuss specific practices in graphic detail. Leave this for the time after you are married. You are turned on by each other. Keep the fire sizzling but don't fan the flame. Move slowly and learn to deal wisely with the hot, emotional magnetism between you both in this engagement period.

In my years as a sex educator, therapist and counsellor, I have taken a number of couples through marriage preparation. When it comes to preparing for a lifetime of the best sex, one of the most important areas a couple needs to explore is how to deal with romantic love and sexual desire in the engagement period.

Understanding the passion: dealing with love and desire

What is this passionate attraction between two people? That in-the-clouds feeling of wanting to see, do things with, make love to—just be with—your beloved? That burst of energy when you see her. That heart-palpitating, pupil-dilating feeling when he walks into the room.

You are fearless; you would do anything, say anything, and fight any battle for your loved one. Your beloved is perfect, faultless, precious … angelic.

These are the feelings of romantic love. And they are the result of changes in your brain that make you focus your energy on one person. You are motivated to pursue this particular person for the reward of intimacy and ownership—you fall in love with him or her.

The Bible recognises the power of romantic love in Song of Songs:

for love is as strong as death, its jealousy unyielding as the grave. It burns like blazing fire, like a mighty flame. Many waters cannot quench love; rivers cannot sweep it away. (8:6b–7a)

Shakespeare wrote of love in *Romeo and Juliet*: 'Love is a smoke made with the fume of sighs. Being purged; a fire sparkling in lovers' eyes, being vexed, a sea nourished with lovers' tears. What is it else? A madness most discreet, a choking gall and a preserving sweet'.

It is fire, it is a sea, it is sweet and bitter ... it is love. And it is brain chemistry!

This falling in love phenomenon[40] is associated with a spray of the chemical dopamine from areas associated with reward and motivation, to the rest of the brain. Other chemical changes include an increase of norepinephrine and a decrease in serotonin. This spray of dopamine leads to a lover's high: focused attention on their loved one, rearrangement of priorities, increased energy and mood swings. The increase in norepinephrine brings on sweating and a pounding heart, emotional dependence and elevated sexual desire. The drop in serotonin causes a mini obsessive-compulsive state with feelings of sexual possessiveness, jealousy, compulsive thinking about him or her, and a craving for emotional union with this one person. All these reactions push up the level of testosterone in the brain and the desire for sexual intimacy with the loved one.

---

40   Fisher, H, Aron, A & Brown, L 2006, 'Romantic love: a mammalian brain system for mate choice', *Philosophical Transactions of the Royal Society Bulletin*, 361, pp. 2173–2186.

Other parts of your brain are also affected. The part of the brain that determines feelings of fear is inhibited, as is the part of the cerebral cortex that influences your judgement. Anyone who has been in the throes of romantic love can understand it: love is fearless. And yes, love is blind.

The power of love is why rejection and failure in love can be truly 'biologically' painful. Being 'in love' is chemically like an addiction or obsession, and therefore loss felt at a neurochemical and whole body level. It can induce clinical depression and, in extreme cases, stalking, homicide and sometimes, even suicide.[41]

The intense power of romantic love is also why we need to take extreme care when we deal with the emotion. Falling in love should come with a 'handle with care' warning.

And that is why the Bible tells us to be aware of how we deal with this emotion. Three times in the Song of Songs (2:7; 3:5; 8:4), the woman exhorts her friends to take care when arousing the passions of desire and love: 'Do not arouse or awaken love until it so desires'.

Fortunately this love-crazed phase lasts only 12–24 months. We wouldn't survive it for much longer than this!

You need to be wise and very cautious in your response to the emotional rollercoaster of falling in love. Love is both *affection* (feeling, emotion) and voluntary *action*. The neurochemical cocktail will draw you to your beloved; you 'fall' in love. You are motivated to pursue the reward of

41   Fisher, H, Aron, A, Brown, L, Strong, G & Mashek, D 2010, 'Reward, addiction, and emotion regulation systems associated with rejection in love', *Journal of Neurophysiology*, 104, pp. 51–60.

intimacy with your loved one. This is the feeling, accompanied by the kick in the gut of testosterone-driven sexual desire, that sends your sex drive into a tail spin.

But, as a human with a higher cerebral control system and the ability to choose your response, what you do to follow up the urge is up to you. You can choose to follow the lustful path of immediate gratification, not caring about the consequences, either for yourself, your partner or anyone else. Or you can stop and let wisdom guide your next action. Loving actions of restraint and other-focused caring when chemicals are screaming for satisfaction is a conscious choice.

When it comes to sex before marriage, this approach of patient waiting seems out of step with society, which works on a 'try before you buy' relationship pattern. The world calls you to follow your feelings. 'If it feels good you should do it.' 'You have a right to happiness.' 'Nobody should tell you not to pursue your personal satisfaction.' 'After all, you are engaged to be married—why wait?'

Look around you. Society's consumerist model to relationships takes many forms. It includes everything from testing out sexual compatibility with a series of casual affairs, to a partly relational 'friends with benefits' status, and cohabitation. These relationships represent a sliding scale of commitment without the 'till death do us part' wedding vows.

God instructs us that 'marriage should be honoured by all, and the marriage bed kept pure' (Hebrews 13:4). Sexual purity and premarital sex are not compatible.

In a sexualised culture, Christian couples sometimes wonder: Does following the world view of cohabitation and premarital sex bring contentment and happiness? All their friends are doing it. And they seem to be having fun. Why should a Christian couple behave differently?

Engaged the world's way

A couple fall in love. They get engaged. And then, in the heat of the moment, engulfed by romantic love and passion, they make love. This is an expression of lust. Lust is an emotion that interprets the feelings of love as an act of self-focused gratification. I want to own you, to possess your body. The result is premarital sexual activity.

What is the long-term outcome of lust?

A report from the Australian Bureau of Statistics[42] tells us that the majority of couples registering their marriage in 2011 cohabited prior to marriage (78.2%). The cohabitation model of relationship places the couple in a pseudo-commitment state. This is a relationship where they agree to a one male–one female, one-flesh relationship while still checking out whether it is possible to live with one another for the long term.

Many young adults cycle between cohabiting partners in the search for lifelong marital partners.[43] This may represent a form of intensive dating that ultimately leads to marriage, perhaps after living with several different partners. However, no study has found a protective influence of cohabitation on marital stability.[44] Instead, many studies link cohabitation to a

42   3310.0—*Marriages and Divorces, Australia, 2011*. Viewed on January 23 2013 at <http://www.abs.gov.au/ausstats/abs@.nsf/Products/3327AE72B9B7BB75CA257AC50 011308D>.
43   Lichter, DT, Turner, RN & Sassler, S 2010, 'National estimates of the rise in serial cohabitation', *Social Science Research*, 39, 5, pp. 754–765.
44   Manning, WD & Cohen, JA 2012, 'Premarital cohabitation and marital dissolution: An examination of recent marriages', *Journal of Marriage and Family*, 74, pp. 377–387.

higher rate of divorce[45] and a lower level of marital quality[46] than for those who had not done so. The research also indicates that men and women differ in the expectations with which they go into a cohabitation relationship.[47] Women are more likely to associate the relationship with love and a step towards marriage, whereas men make the association with sex and not necessarily a prequel to marriage.

Researchers surveying more than 2000 couples tell us that the longer a couple waits to become sexually involved the more likely they are to have better quality sex, better relationship communication, higher levels of relationship satisfaction and higher perceived relationship stability in marriage.[48] They suggest that couples who 'prioritise sex promptly at the outset of a relationship often find their relationships underdeveloped when it comes to the qualities that make relationships stable and spouses reliable and trustworthy'. This should be no surprise. When physical intimacy is the only bond between couples, the communication that forms the foundation for a long-term relationship is underdeveloped at best and, more often, non-existent.

45   Jose, A, O'Leary, DK & Moyer, A 2010, 'Does premarital cohabitation predict subsequent marital stability and marital quality? A meta-analysis', *Journal of Marriage and Family*, 72, pp. 105–116.

46   Andrews, K 2012, *Maybe I Do: Modern Marriage & The Pursuit of Happiness*, Conner Court Publishing, Australia, pp. 198–218.

47   Huang, PM, Smock, PJ, Manning, WD & Bergstrom-Lynch, CA 2011, 'He says, she says: Gender and cohabitation', *Journal of Family Issues*, 32, 7, pp. 876–905.

48   Busby, DM, Carroll, JS & Willoughby, BJ 2010, 'Compatibility or restraint? The effects of sexual timing on marriage relationships', *Journal of Family Psychology*, 24, 6, pp. 766–774. See also Busby, DM, Carroll, JS & Willoughby, BJ 2010, 'Differing relationship outcomes when sex happens before, on, or after first dates', *Journal of Sex Research*, 0 (0) pp. 1–10. Available on line at <http://www.tandfonline.com/doi/abs/10.1080/00224499.2 012.714012?journalCode=hjsr20#preview>.

In today's culture where individual freedom, autonomy and self-fulfilment are the norm, it seems that in a cohabitation relationship, many women barter sex to get love and a wedding band, and men give love for the convenience of a regular sexual partner. Sex has become the ultimate commodity.

Engaged God's way

The Bible clearly tells us to wait until marriage for sexual intimacy (Hebrews 13:4) and it repeatedly calls on God's people to refrain from sexual immorality (Matthew 15:18–20; Romans 13:12–14; 1 Corinthians 6:17–19; and others). In the midst of the world's plethora of seductive sexual offerings, the Bible tells us that sexual purity is an essential characteristic for holiness.

Remember, holiness means being special—being set apart for God. When it comes to sex, this does not mean we have to avoid sexual activity. Sex in itself is not unholy; God invented it. It is God's gift to us. Sexual holiness means conducting our sexuality in a way that honours and pleases God: one man and one woman using sex to serve each other in a lifelong committed marriage. This is what it means to use our sexuality to worship God. It involves abstaining from sexual activities until marriage; and, within marriage, using sex to serve our partner, not just please ourselves.

How should you behave sexually as an engaged couple?

Let's start with what you are looking forward to in marriage. Sex in marriage is part of a lifelong, naked and no-shame relationship of total and unabashed trust. To prepare for this, the period of engagement becomes the training ground for trustworthiness and other-focused loving. The things we do when we are single men and women in the engagement period lay the very foundations of character that make us godly husbands and wives. Engagement is a time when couples should learn to:

- deal carefully with sexual desire
- set wise boundaries for intimate behaviour.

Dealing carefully with sexual desire

Testosterone runs high when you are in love. Recognise this. Accept it as God's gift to you and resist the temptation to allow it to overwhelm you and develop into lust. How do you do this?

❤ Discipline your sexual urges and fantasies

Being in love will fill your mind with your loved one when you are not together. This is normal and healthy. However, be careful *how you think* about your future husband or wife.

What actions and activities do you think about when you imagine the two of you together?

In Romans 6:11–13, Paul urges us to 'not let sin reign in your mortal body so that you obey its evil desires'. Rather he tells us 'offer every part of yourself to him [God] as an instrument of righteousness'. In fact, he exhorts the Colossians (3:5) to actively put these desires that belong to our earthly nature (sexual immorality, impurity, lust, evil desires) to death.

Keeping your sexual thoughts pure is not easy when your brain is flooded with testosterone. It will be made harder if you have been sexually active before. It will be even more difficult if you have been or are currently using pornography, reading erotic novels or feeding yourself on sex-filled videos and television.

As an engaged couple you must be aware of the temptation to think lustfully of your fiancé or fiancée, and be ever vigilant. As the Apostle Peter advises, we need to be constantly alert, informed and fully sober if we want to be countercultural in how we think (1 Peter 1:13–15). So, when a sexual thought comes into your mind, don't dwell on it and build it up to a lustful fantasy. Instead, banish it and replace it with wholesome and pure thoughts of him or her. Follow Paul's exhortation to the Philippians (4:8) to think only on those things that are true, noble, right, pure, whatever is lovely and admirable.

Don't feel ashamed and guilty when sexual thoughts enter your mind. Even Paul said he had to beat or pummel his body and make it his slave (1 Corinthians 9:25–27). Persevere. Train your thinking. It may not happen overnight, but it will happen. When you are married, you can pick up on the thoughts and let your sensuality loose—together.

Sometimes, especially in a long period of engagement, the craving can be severe. Get help. Find an older married person you trust—a man if you're a guy and a woman if you're a girl. Share your thoughts and feelings with them. Meet, pray and be accountable to them. Meditate on the Bible passages above and others like it.[49] They will help you to fence in your fantasies.

♥ Avoid temptation

Resisting the urge to put lustful thoughts into action becomes difficult when you are together. Faced with the one you love, dopamine floods your brain and your cerebral

49   See Matthew 15:18–20; Romans 13:12–14; 1 Corinthians 6:17–19; Colossians 3:2–8.

control systems are at an all-time low. You long to have your beloved in your life—and in your bed.

The fact that you know you shouldn't do it sends a frisson of norepinephrine-induced exhilaration spiralling through you. The high stress emotion of 'the forbidden' lures you to follow the seductive desire for sexual intimacy and premarital sex.

Recognise what is happening to you. You are being tempted to lose self-control. To allow the 'heat of the moment' need for immediate self-gratification to overrule God's instruction for self-control. You are feeling enticed to take that first step onto the sexual intimacy slippery slope. Keep alert. And be aware of the external factors that encourage you to lower your guard. Sometimes it might be the non-Christian friends you spend time with. Peer pressure is powerful. Avoid alcohol and drugs, which act at brain level to lower inhibitions and allow desire free reign. Stay sober-minded and in control of your emotions. Resist the devil's lies (James 4:7; 1 Peter 5:8–9).

Step back. Take the emotional equivalent of a cold shower. Recognise the power of your feelings. Don't feel guilty or ashamed for feeling the way you do. It's perfectly normal. It is God's blessing to get you ready for the sexual intimacy that will complete your marriage. It is powerful for a purpose—at the right time and in the context of marriage.

Paul tells us how to resist these powerful temptations (Ephesians 6:10–12). So get your spiritual armour on. How you behave towards each other as fiancé and fiancée will set the foundation for your marriage life as husband and wife. Nurture your love and delight in each other by practising self-control, patience and other-focused caring. Feast together on the fruits of the Spirit (Galatians 5:22–23).

Turn the moments of high sexual feeling into shared learning experiences. Tell your fiancé or fiancée how you are feeling and, importantly, what happened to turn you on. He or she may not recognise that touching you in some way or stroking that part of your body, saying something, or even giving you a particular look sent your hormones spiralling. Share it. Draw on the weapons and safety net of the armour of God to resist the temptation. Then, save that arousal experience for a special honeymoon moment when you can enjoy unfettered sexual intimacy.

But, what is the boundary between the 'getting to know you' activities during the engagement period and the unfettered sexual intimacy of marriage? Is there a specific act? Or is there flexibility?

Sexual intimacy: setting boundaries for sensuality

Does avoiding premarital sexual activity mean that you shouldn't kiss? Or touch? Or maybe that's OK and you just shouldn't go as far as genital touching and oral sex? On the other hand, maybe all that's all right, just as long as you don't have sexual intercourse?

I don't want to be legalistic. Rather I want to challenge you to wisdom in making decisions and setting boundaries in lovemaking. So, I'm giving you a few principles to follow.

Firstly, from the Apostle Paul's words, learn to see sex for what it is:

'I have the right to do anything', you say—but not everything is beneficial. 'I have the right to do anything'—but I will not be mastered by anything. You say, 'Food for the stomach and the stomach for food,

and God will destroy them both'. The body, however, is not meant for sexual immorality but for the Lord, and the Lord for the body. (1 Corinthians 6:12–13)

Recognise sex as a gift from God. Use it not as a right but as a blessing, to be saved for and enjoyed in marriage. Acknowledge it for what it is: important, but a part of the whole range of blessings God gives us in marriage. **Don't idolise sex.** In the Bible, eating food sacrificed to idols and committing sexual immorality are bracketed together (Acts 15:20, 29).

Secondly, let your actions be a joint decision. **Discuss sexual boundaries with your partner**. Be honest. Follow up on the earlier point we discussed about identifying what personally turns you on. Recognise that you are two individuals who differ in more ways than just your gender! What turns you on sexually differs. You may find that some action you deem ordinary is a total turn-on to your partner. Use this conversation to set boundaries for sexual activities. It may mean that you need to discuss when and where you will be alone together. Even what items of clothing you would wear (or not) and how and what part of the body you touch.

A rule of thumb in setting couple behaviour boundaries is to ask yourself: Is what you are doing as a couple something you would be comfortable sharing with your Bible study group? Would it be mutually edifying? If so, go for it.

Be accountable for what happens. Have an older married couple who you can talk to. They will continue to be invaluable when you need a helping hand as newlyweds.

Use self-control in sexual intimacy as a training ground for trustworthiness. Marriage is a naked and no-shame relationship for the rest of your life. To be naked before another person is to be ultimately vulnerable. And to feel no shame in this act of shared intimacy is an act of trust. How does this work out practically? Learn to be **other-focused in all your actions**. Learn to control your own desires and help your fiancé or fiancée deal with theirs. In the spirit of putting his or her needs before yours, build each other up in purity. Practise 1 Corinthians 13 love. Your love will not be one of self-seeking for personal sexual gratification. Rather, it will seek to honour, protect and persevere in building up the other for the time when you can share the wonderful intimacies of marriage.

Don't be ashamed to tell your friends why you have decided to save sexual intimacy for marriage. Jesus instructed his disciples to be as wise as serpents and as innocent as doves (Matthew 10:16). When your non-Christian friends speak of sexual desire as an uncontrollable force that must be sated, tell them that what you feel for your loved one is too precious to be abused. Talk to them of the passionate joys of a lifetime of good sex that you plan to have in a committed relationship of total trust. Do it as the Apostle Peter says, with courtesy and respect, keeping a good conscience, so that those who slander your good conduct in Christ may be put to shame when they accuse you (1 Peter 3:15–16). Dare to be different and set a counterculture of sexual purity.

What if?

Some of you may have already given in to the temptation to have sexual intercourse, either with the person you are engaged to or someone else. Or maybe you haven't had sexual intercourse but have come close—so close that you feel ashamed and guilty. On the other hand you might have given in to lust and watched pornography. Or you may masturbate regularly and feel bad about it. Some of you may have even been sinned against—a victim of sexual abuse or rape. You may have discussed this with someone. But more likely it is your secret, and hiding it makes you feel dirty and ashamed, or hurt and angry about what was done to you—even angry at a God who let this happen.

Yes, whether by your choice or circumstances outside your control, what happened is wrong. But you shouldn't feel ashamed and guilty about it. Turn your emotions around and rethink your sexuality and relationship with your future spouse. Thoughtfully and prayerfully turn your sex life over to God. Claim the promise that repentance brings. Remember, Christ came and died for broken people.

Having listed a range of sexual and other sins, Paul goes on to say:

> And that is what some of you were. But you were washed, you were sanctified, you were justified in the name of the Lord Jesus Christ and by the Spirit of our God. (1 Corinthians 6:11)

Trust this promise of sanctification and let the sin go. Then move on to set a new way of thinking, living and relating as a couple as you plan your married life together. Consider the sins of the past dead and yourself alive in Christ (Romans 6:10–14).

This letting go and moving on with Christ as a new creation takes effort and time. Specific situations need to be dealt with wisely. How much detail should you expose to your partner?

What about your sexual experiences before you met? How explicit should you be? What of abusive experiences? Rape? There is no easy answer to these questions. You may need help from a wise elder or a counsellor. Don't be afraid to ask for assistance. You owe it to your partner and to the success of your marriage. You can depend on the God who created you to see you through. As Paul told the Romans, nothing will separate you from God's love for you (Romans 8:37–39). It is best to face it and deal with it.

As a Christian sex therapist, I see newly married and not-so-newly married Christian couples who carry the burden of shame, guilt and the anger of unresolved sexual issues. They present in my consultation room anxious and hurting. They tell me of sexual desire and arousal problems that threaten to destroy their marital sexual intimacy. We spend time teasing out the sexual issues in their history that are acting as stumbling blocks. It takes time, effort and grace, but good sex does happen. So, if you have any doubts or anxieties about sexual experiences or behaviour, talk to a therapist or counsellor. Do it early. Give yourself and your future spouse time to deal with the issues before marriage.

Another 'what if' involves masturbation: Is it wrong to masturbate during this engagement period?

Masturbation, 'jerking off'—call it what you may—solo sex is self-stimulation of the genitals (or sometimes other erogenous parts of the body like the breasts) to orgasm (and ejaculation in the man). An orgasm releases feel-good chemicals in the brain. Dopamine and endorphins give a thrilling brain buzz and oxytocin causes the feelings of relaxation and euphoria. We don't have clear statistics, but therapists tell us that 90% of men say that they masturbate and the other 10% are probably lying. The statistics are even harder to come by for women. But we know that they too masturbate.

Historically, masturbation has been seen as a display of 'loss': a loss of self-control over a man's own nature and thereby an undermining of masculinity[50]; a loss of essential energy and creative potential. The biblical story of Onan[51] has been seen to describe masturbation as a turning away from divine guidance (from where comes the term 'Onanism'). However this story needs to be interpreted with care, since it is really about disobeying God or, at the most, coitus interruptus and not masturbation at all.

Historically, the fear of 'loss' and the consequences for general and mental health in particular led to a search for a 'cure' for the condition. These have taken the forms of food, medicines and even surgical equipment. Over the ages, a range of torture-inducing equipment was developed and used to subdue the urge to masturbate.[52] In 1837, health food enthusiast Sylvester Graham is said to have preached sermons about the dangers of masturbation, and invented a cracker to help ward off those dangers. If you ate your cracker in the morning, the blandness of the cracker was supposed to lower your lust all day so that you would not have 'vital fluid expending' urges. Similarly, Dr John Henry Kellogg believed that spicy and sweet foods would increase the libido. When

50   Garlick, S 2012, 'Masculinity, pornography, and the history of masturbation', *Sexuality & Culture*, 16, 3, pp. 306–332.
51   Genesis 38:7–10
52   See <http://www.ranker.com/list/top-10-most-brutal-anti-masturbation-devices/robert-wabash?page=1>.

cornflakes were invented, Kellogg immediately latched onto its possibility as a sex-reducing staple food because of its lack of spiciness and general lack of flavour. The next time you reach for a cracker or a bowl of cornflakes, know that they were both used as a cure for masturbation!

The search for a cure continues, with the internet rife with websites that offer herbal cures for masturbation and nocturnal emissions (wet dreams). There is, however, no empirical evidence that any of these work other than at a purely psychological level.

So, what's the big deal with masturbation? After all, it is a great tension release and it doesn't harm anyone. Or does it?

Here's the catch: it is near impossible to masturbate without some form of erotic thoughts. In the engagement period these thoughts could be of your partner. On the other hand, they could be of some other person, a porn star or a sexual situation.

If you are masturbating to thoughts of the person you are engaged to, and this involves lustful fantasies of sexual acts, you are reducing your future marriage partner to a commodity for your personal gratification. It will be near impossible to shut these thoughts out when you are next together. This could lead to your desiring to play out your fantasies with your partner and, ultimately, to inappropriate sexual intimacy, even intercourse. This in turn could result in shame and guilt, and could lead to problems in your marital sex life, a vicious cycle of marred sexual intimacy.

What about masturbation as an outlet for sexual tension (like when you go home after seeing your partner)? In this situation the question is one of self-control. If you get into a habit of masturbating whenever you're sexually aroused, you're getting into a habit of poor self-control. Self-control is one of the gifts of the Spirit (Galatians 5:23). God wants us to learn to control our body, not indulge in passionate lust (1 Thessalonians 4:3–5). Being sexually aroused doesn't have to lead to orgasm. You don't have to masturbate. You can do something to distract yourself, or channel your energy into some other productive activity. Exercise, good music and even a cup of hot chocolate or strong coffee send up endorphins and other brain chemicals which, while not being the same as an orgasmic high, come pretty close.

We have discussed how important self-control is in terms of training yourself to be trustworthy during the engagement period. This will continue into marriage. Your husband or wife is not always going to feel like sex when you want it. If you're used to controlling yourself, you'll avoid becoming a slave to the need for immediate gratification. But if you're used to quickly masturbating to satisfy your desire, then you are likely to pressure your spouse for sex or watch pornography, both of which will erode your partner's trust and damage your marriage relationship.

Regular masturbation to pornography or some other sexual activity can also set up patterns of quick sexual response in your brain. You may carry these into your marriage and find difficulty with intimacy and sexual performance in marriage.

What if you come (climax, have an orgasm) when you are together as an engaged couple? Maybe not doing anything more complex than a hug? Is that masturbation? Is it a sin? It is a normal physiological response of your body to being close to the one you love. It is not lust and definitely not masturbation. Don't feel ashamed or guilty if it happens.

Some of you reading this may be in the habit of masturbating regularly. Right now you may be feeling pretty awful. Stop worrying. It's a habit that can be changed. Here are some techniques that could help:

1. Keep track of the triggers that tempt you to masturbate. Is it some place? Some thought? Avoid these places and redirect the thoughts as they come into your conscience.
2. Find some alternative activity. If coming home to your single room after visiting your fiancée or fiancé makes you want to masturbate, schedule in an alternate activity at that time. Maybe a session at the gym or a chat with a friend may help.
3. Find an older wiser Christian who can be your mentor.

The time you spend together as an engaged couple is important. Use it wisely. Train your body and mind to be self-controlled and loving—other-focused in your passions and wants. And look forward to a lifetime of good sex as a couple.

A proviso to purity

We finish this section with a word of caution.

Sexual purity during the engagement period is an act of honouring your future spouse and a witness of your belief in marriage as the appropriate and God-given context for sex. However, avoiding sexual intimacy before marriage does not automatically assure you of great sex and mind-blowing orgasms as soon as you get married. This is a myth and an impossible expectation. What marriage promises is the best relationship ever. Great sex takes time and practice. We will discuss this in the next chapter.

Take-away messages

- The engagement period is a time when a couple get to know each other intimately but not sexually.
- Communication is important. Share your expectations and anxieties. Ask for help if you need to.
- Be careful how you deal with the intense passion of romantic love. Be wise in the choices you make.
- The engagement period is the training ground for trustworthiness and other-focused loving. Make it a habit.
- Practise sexual purity in your thoughts (fantasies) and your actions.
- Learn what your body looks like and how it responds. Learn how this is different to that of your fiancé/fiancée and look forward to the intimacy of discovery once you are married.

Chapter 6
Honeymoon sexpectations

The honeymoon: those halcyon days in a secluded resort and then the romantic haze-filled months of new love that follow. In this section we will explore the wedding night and those first few months of marriage: that time of sexpectation.

The wedding ceremony is the culmination of months, maybe even years, of planning. Family and friends unstintingly give of their time, sometimes even their money, so the wedding can be just the way the couple have wanted it to be—perfect.

Then, after the ceremony and the speeches and the drive away from the reception in the car with 'just married' painted on the back, the couple is off on their honeymoon. They look forward to being alone, undisturbed. They are staring at life together—just the two of them.

Finally, their every dream and fantasy is about to come true ...

Sara watches him as he slips his shirt off. She has never seen him naked. She has in fact never seen any man naked! Daniel has the most beautiful body. She feels a frisson of excitement and then, as he moves towards her, a cloud of oppressive anxiety. She is very, very tired. Suddenly all she wants is a hot bath. And then to roll into bed … and sleep. But that would disappoint her husband. He has been so self-controlled and patient through the engagement time. He always did the right thing, stopping and moving away when she pressed him to go a little further. She knows he's been waiting to touch her, kiss her, to have sex. And she so wants to live up to his expectations tonight.

And so, she moves into his arms. She smiles at him lovingly, wanting to be the hot woman he expects her to be.

Daniel pushes the straps off her shoulders. The silk clings to her skin, then slips off her body and pools at her feet. His arms tighten around her as he bends his face to hers. His lips tease hers and she opens her mouth to him. She has fantasised about this so often. But somehow the reality is different. She feels his erection press on her thigh. His kisses deepen. They are both naked in bed. His penis is pushing against her. Pain shoots to her brain.

'Relax darling', Daniel whispers. She can't. It hurts too much. He comes outside her. Rolls over and holds her as she sobs.

Surely, it is not supposed to be this way …

Sam is the happiest he has ever been. Finally, tonight Stephanie will be his. They have waited so long for this day. He has kept his distance. Maintained the boundaries they set together. Sometimes he would get so excited that he would come when they were kissing. She was so innocent, she didn't even notice. Only his mentor from church knows about his struggles with masturbation and pornography.

Stephanie comes out of the bathroom in a sexy little piece of lacy lingerie. She looks and smells heavenly. Their eyes meet. As she moves into his arms and their lips and tongues meet and explore, he knows it has all been worth the wait. They push their clothes off each other and fall on the bed. She is wet and ready. He fumbles as he places himself between her legs. He tries to remember the pictures he looked at on the internet— what he is supposed to do. And then the unthinkable happens. He comes. And he loses his erection. It happens before he can even enter her. He is mortified and angry at himself. He looks into her tear-filled eyes. 'I'm sorry.'

Surely, it is not supposed to be this way ...

Tonight they will consummate their love for each other. They have been together as a couple from high school. Six years including the two years' engagement while they saved money and got their careers on track. They have followed the advice of the youth leaders and pastors—stayed pure, not lusted for each other, not touched. Well, not too much.

But, as he holds her, James' thoughts stray to the others: the girls he fantasised about during the time he was engaged to Eva, the times when he was so turned on he thought he would burst if he didn't do something, those images he looked at on the internet when he couldn't stand the tension. He turns his face away from Eva. Surely she will see it in his eyes. He feels guilty, ashamed and horrible.

Surely, it is not supposed to be this way ...

Emily and Zac shower together. They are happy to be finally married. They giggle as they soap each other. Their parents and church friends believed that they were both virgins. Only their friends at work knew that they'd been having sex for the last six months. Zac towels himself and walks nude across the room to the minibar. Emily puts on the frothy white lace negligee her sister had given her as a wedding present. 'Hey, want something to drink?' Zac glances back at her. 'Since when do you dress up for bed?' he laughs and swipes at her bottom.

'I wanted today to be special', she whispers. Zac scratches his head. 'We're married now baby. No need for the seduction routine. Anyway I'm washed out.' Emily looks at Zac, wanting to feel hot and wet for him … but feeling … nothing.

Later that night, Emily lies in bed. What has happened to the Zac who showered her with compliments and teased her into sexual arousal? What happened to their sizzling lovemaking?

Surely, it is not supposed to be this way …

Jessica cradles the cup of coffee in her hands. John has returned early from work tonight. He will expect to make love—again. She will have to pretend she wants to—again.

Jessica thinks back to the time when they were engaged. She had so wanted him to touch her, to kiss her. She was the one who had wanted more. He was the one who held back. And then there was the honeymoon night. She had expected it to be wonderful, exciting. Instead it had been clumsy, uncomfortable, and even painful. And now, two months into their married life, she just doesn't want to do it.

Surely, it is not supposed to be this way …

Maybe your wedding night and the months that followed were not quite the disaster it was for these couples. Maybe you had a good start to your sexual relationship on your honeymoon—well, a little messy, but better than you expected. Or, you may have some other story of honeymoon sexual misadventure that we haven't described here. Whatever the hiccup, be assured that you are in the majority: most couples have a rocky start to their sex life.

In his book *Marriage: Sex in the Service of God*, Christopher Ash defines marriage as a 'voluntary sexual and public social union of one man and one woman from different families. This union is patterned upon the union of God with his people, his bride, the Christ with his Church. Intrinsic to this union is God's calling to lifelong exclusive sexual faithfulness'.[53]

As husband and wife, you have voluntarily made a public declaration before God and his people. You have promised to be committed and faithful to one another in a wonderful one-flesh sexual union, beginning with your honeymoon. You are at the starting point of a journey in which you will explore the God-given gift of joyful sex. The honeymoon is the *beginning*. It is important to remember this. Marriage is a journey of exploration and growth in all aspects of relationship. Your sex life as a couple will deepen and improve as you explore what you and your partner like and dislike. This is a lifelong process of other-focused loving and total trust and faith in your spouse.

As a couple you need to understand this. Clear your minds of the media and internet-driven world view of sex as an instant, all-

53   Ash, C 2003, *Marriage: Sex in the Service of God*, Regent College Publishing, Vancouver, pp. 63.

consuming brain explosion of mutual orgasmic satisfaction. Let go of feelings of shame and guilt, of past thoughts and experiences. Physical sexual intimacy is a seed that you as a couple plant during your honeymoon. It is a special God-given gift, private to the two of you, one you will water and nurture with patient love and care as you live together. It will grow and give you the fragrant results that the lovers extol in Song of Songs (for example, 4:10–11).

Many couples don't understand this. They expect instant results. The experience of sex during the honeymoon and the first months, sometimes even for years after marriage, fails dismally to live up to their expectations. Some struggle on. Others give up and lead a life together devoid of true sexual intimacy, or sometimes even devoid of all intimacy—an asexual marriage.

In the next section we will look at some of the common reasons for sexual problems in the first few months of marriage, and how starting sexual intimacy based on God's pattern for relationship lays the foundation for the best sex for life.

Sexpectations and misconceptions
Here are some of the more common misconceptions we see. Many of these are played out in the couples' scenarios above.

1. Sex will be perfect on your wedding night
What could possibly go wrong? Making love looks so simple in the movies and romantic novels. Girl meets boy. They fall in love. There is deep passionate kissing as they stumble toward the bedroom. Their clothes lie scattered along the way. They fall into bed. They have mind-blowing sex and simultaneous orgasms. Soon they are at it again, and again … and so on.

This is the fantasy, one that all the couples in our scenarios have read about and watched on television and in movies. The reality is that this rarely, if ever, happens.

Marriage brings together two fallen people with very different attitudes, values and expectations of sex. If they are both virgins, any knowledge they have of the genitals and sexual arousal is purely theoretical. On the wedding night both are tired, stressed and anxious. Further, as young Christian people, they have been nurtured in the godly values of sexual purity until marriage. Now, with the wedding ring on the finger, couples expect to suddenly turn from self-controlled gentle lovers into sexual Olympians. Sorry, that's unlikely to happen.

On the other hand, if you are a girl, you may be labouring under a further sexpectation that your first sexual intercourse experience will be very traumatic and you are likely to tear or bleed. Perhaps someone told you that it is your duty to put up with the discomfort because your husband will expect intercourse. You might be afraid and may be even faintly resentful. The first sight of an erect penis does little to allay these fears. Sometimes this anxiety and fear could cause the muscles around the vagina (the pubococcygeus) to contract, making it difficult, even impossible, for the penis to enter. This reinforces the fear and sets up a vicious cycle. This condition, known as vaginismus is more common than people might think. It is probably what happened to Sara.

The husband, in the spirit of male leadership, thinks that he is expected to know what to do and how to make this first experience arousing and memorable for them both. He has been waiting a long time for this. And he wants so much to do well for his wife for their first time together. This pressure to perform may well make him anxious and uptight, resulting in him coming too soon or even losing his erection. Sam is probably suffering from this form of performance anxiety.

You can see how a perfect act of sexual intercourse under these high-stress, high-expectation circumstances is like expecting someone to swim in the Olympics on their first swimming lesson!

In case you are thinking that this is a reason to have sex before marriage, the truth is that first-time sex is rarely easy or perfectly comfortable for either the man or the woman, whether or not they are married.[54] In fact, premarital situations of first sex often result in regret and sadness. So don't put too many expectations on 'that first time' event.

What should you do?

Basically, take it easy and relax. Remember, your wedding night is the beginning of an exciting sexual journey. You are in this together and for a lifetime. It is OK to be uncertain, to fumble, to laugh—even cry.

Here are a few first night tips.

♥ Take time to get to know each other's body

The genitalia of the opposite sex are a mystery even to those who have a PhD in anatomy. Use the diagrams in the earlier section of the book and conduct a shared 'show and tell'. Remember, you are now entering the 'naked and no-shame' phase of your life. This means you can be naked together without embarrassment and definitely without fear of rejection. Yes, it is a time of particular vulnerability. You

54   Sprecher, S, Barbee, A & Schwartz, P 1995, 'Was it good for you, too?': Gender differences in first sexual intercourse experiences', *The Journal of Sex Research*, Vol. 32, No. 1, pp. 3–15.

may think that some part of your body isn't attractive, or too small, or too droopy or wrinkly. The point is that, in this special one man–one woman covenant of trust, it is OK to be vulnerable and to accept each other just as you are.

Take your time. Talk about your feelings. It doesn't matter if exploration and touching is all you do on the first night—or the second, or even later in your honeymoon! You have a lifetime together to enjoy good sex.

♥ Enjoy the journey

Be mindful of your feelings at the moment of sharing. Revel in the sensuality. Sexual intimacy is more—far more—than intercourse. There are the senses to be shared. Some are obvious, like touch and smell. Other sensations like taste, sight and sound are often forgotten. Why turn the light off and close our eyes when making love? Why not talk? Laugh together? 'Sensual discovery pathway for couples' (Appendix 2) is an activity I suggest to couples who need to work on the intimacy and sensuality of their marriage. You may find it useful to read this. In 1 Corinthians 7:2–6, Paul tells us that as husband and wife our bodies are joined—bonded together for the purpose of serving and pleasuring the other. Take the first steps carefully. You are setting the pattern for the best sex for life.

♥ Talk about your feelings and fears

You may think that you have said all there is to say during the time of your engagement. But there will be things about sex and intimacy that were just too hard to talk about at that time. Now you are married and you have promised to love, honour and cherish each other. There are life experiences that may affect your intimacy as a couple. Some of these may have come up when you did your marriage preparation. Use this private honeymoon time to talk about these things. How do you feel about various acts of sexual intimacy? Oral sex? Touching each other's genitals? Taking a shower together? Being openly naked? Talking about these can be an erotic adventure in itself. Then try them out! Be gentle with yourself and your partner. But do it. Remember you are setting the foundations for honest and open communication for the future.

2. First intercourse should be romantic and wonderful

You may have dreams of your first sexual experience being romantic and pretty. But in fact, first sexual intercourse can be awkward (you don't instinctively know how everything works). Sometimes it can be a little fearful (How can this rather large erect penis actually fit into that little vaginal opening?). And yes, sometimes it's messy (semen and vaginal secretions can be plentiful) and even painful.

Let's look at the wife. If the woman is a virgin and has not used a tampon or had a vaginal examination done by a doctor, she is likely to have some discomfort when the penis pushes in. She may even feel some pain and bleed a little. The bleeding is from the tearing of the hymen. Not all women bleed; in fact only about 50% do. So bleeding on first intercourse is definitely not a sign of virginity.

The discomfort comes from the breaking of the hymen as well as from the muscles (pubococcygeus) around the vagina instinctively contracting around the penis as it pushes in. This is exacerbated when the woman is not sufficiently relaxed, lubricated and ready for sex.

Sometimes the pain can be very severe, like it was for Sara. The technical term for this sort of vulvar and pelvic pain associated with sexual intercourse is dyspareunia. Sometimes this pain can be due to an infection. However, as sex therapists, what we commonly see in young newly-married virgins is a condition called vaginismus.

Vaginismus is for real. It is *not* something in the woman's head. And it is definitely *not* because the girl is selfishly avoiding sex with her spouse. In this condition the pelvic floor muscles involuntarily contract at attempted penetration by the penis, despite the woman's expressed wish for sex. Some women experience thigh and abdominal muscle contraction as well. These contractions are associated with varying degrees of fear of pain and penetration. Most of these women have desire for their partner and evidence of sexual arousal in vaginal moisture and swelling. As such it is a very distressing condition for both the woman and her husband.

The most common cause for vaginismus in a young newlywed couple is poor information and incorrect assumptions about sex and sexual behaviour. Many of the Christian couples I see in my practice have rarely been given premarital sex information and are ignorant of the differences in the male and female sexual response (described earlier). In addition, sexual beliefs and behaviour patterns in many of the young men I see are influenced by pornography and masturbatory habits. The sorrow and mutual anxiety the couple feel at their failure to consummate their marriage, and their helplessness in not knowing what to do about it, exacerbates the condition as they repeatedly try and fail. After a while they stop trying. This leads to a decrease in mutual sexual desire and relational tensions. Sometimes this results in a sexless marriage. Sex therapists see some couples only when they desperately want a pregnancy.

The condition is sometimes made worse by well-meaning friends and even clergy who frame the problem in terms of the girl selfishly refusing sex to her spouse. And call her to serve him by being a desiring and desirous sexual partner. The problem is that most times this is exactly what she wants to be, but her pelvic muscles don't obey.

Vaginismus is treatable. It is important that the couple goes to a sex therapist or counsellor as soon as possible. In my experience, the treatment increases intimacy and brings couples closer together.

What about the man? Can first sex be painful for him? Yes, it sometimes can. The tip of a man's penis, called the glans, is very sensitive. It's covered by a fold of skin called the foreskin and held down by a band of tissue called the frenulum. This foreskin is cut off if the boy has had the surgical procedure of circumcision. In some uncircumcised boys, the foreskin may be tight and get pushed back in first intercourse. If this happens, it may hurt and the foreskin might tear and bleed. Or else the frenulum may be split and hurt during the friction of intercourse.

Another cause for pain is inflammation of the urine tube (urethra) and the bladder. These conditions, called urethritis and cystitis respectively, are more common in women. The vagina and the urethra are closely attached in a woman. The friction caused by the penis in the vagina could cause some bacteria (normal for the vulva region) to be pushed up into the bladder.

What should you do?

Be prepared. Be patient. You have the rest of your life as a couple to enjoy good sex. Pain and discomfort early in lovemaking can set up reactions in your genitals that may take time and effort to change. You could actually scare your genitals and confuse your brain with a bad start at sexual intimacy!

Prepare yourself. Have a bath, preferably together. Make sure you pass urine before and after sex to minimise the chance of inflammation and cystitis. Take it easy. You are a couple chosen and blessed by God (Colossians 3:12), holy and dearly loved by him. What better place to start practising the characteristics of compassion, kindness, humility, gentleness and patience than in your honeymoon bed? Take the time to arouse each other sexually before sexual intercourse. As a man, make sure your wife is relaxed, her vagina moist and ready. Make sure the penis foreskin is pliant and retractable. Work this into your lovemaking. Have a good lubricant nearby or use saliva as a lubricant.

It truly doesn't matter if you don't consummate your marriage with sexual intercourse on your wedding night—or even on your honeymoon. And if you continue to have pain or difficulty with sexual intercourse, please speak to someone. Talk first to a parent or trusted older couple at church, and then your general practitioner or sex therapist.

3. Prior sexual experiences have no effect on what happens on the honeymoon

You and your spouse are two very different people. Even if you are from the same church, social and ethnic group, you are two individuals from two families who have chosen to leave your family and be united (Genesis 2:24) as man and wife. Your prior experiences matter when it comes to sex.

You may come from a family where intimacy was a way of life; your parents hugged and kissed. Or you may come from one where sex was a swear word, one where there were no overt demonstrations of affection. You may have had good and honest sex education from your parents, church and school, or none at all. Crude jokes from your friends and pornography may have been all the sex education you've had. Maybe you had never been sexually intimate before you met your spouse. On the other hand, you may have been sexually active by choice, like Emily and Zac. Or you may have had other relationships before you met your marriage partner. Masturbation may have been your sexual outlet. Or maybe you were date-raped or sexually abused.

Every one of these situations, and many others, will affect how you seek out and respond to your partner sexually.

♥ Flashbacks

Your brain has an immense storage capacity. Millions of pictures and experiences are kept in the hard drive of your memory. They lie there until, suddenly, there is a trigger that opens that particular file and it's back in the forefront of your consciousness. Prior sexual experiences act this way. Let's go back to our scenarios.

James in the scenario at the start of this chapter had flashbacks of his premarital fantasies. James had also rewired his desire circuits with pornography. Intimacy with his wife pulled up these memories of sexual images and pornographic experiences.

Sara felt 'a cloud of oppressive anxiety' as Daniel stripped. Her pelvic muscles contracted and she could not have sexual intercourse. This anxiety could have been triggered by a lack of education and preparation, or by false stories of pain and trauma. But it is also possible that she had flashbacks from unwanted sexual abuse.

♥ Unrealistic anticipations

The use of pornography replaces reality with fantasy images. And no matter how beautiful and sexy your wife may be, the porn star probably had bigger breasts and smoother pubes. However well-endowed your husband is, the men in erotic novels are bigger and their erections last longer. So you find yourself, often unwillingly, comparing your spouse with the fantasy. You may find yourself thinking about the sexual practices you have seen in porn movies—the anal sex and deviant practices. And you may be tempted to ask your spouse for these activities. You must remember that some men and women are uncomfortable with particular sexual practices, even some that you may consider a normal part of a sexual repertoire, like oral sex or mutual genital touching. So, talk with your spouse about what sexual activities they like and dislike. Do it before you start your lovemaking, and respect their wishes. Put away thoughts of extreme sexual activities and consider your spouse's comfort and desires.

♥ Brain and body reflexes

Some premarital sexual activities set up patterns of response in your body. We call these reflexes. In some males, masturbation—whether accompanied by a fantasy or while watching pornography—sets up the reflex of rapid ejaculation. Their brain gets programmed to achieve an erection and ejaculate to orgasm quickly. Men masturbate for the quick thrill of the dopamine-induced buzz and oxytocin- and endorphin-induced euphoria. Quick is the key; who wants to go on for five … ten … 30 minutes seated at the computer watching pornography? The same programming happens in men who visit sex workers. The sex worker has a set time and the man has to be done and out. This condition, where the man comes fast, is known as premature ejaculation. It can be frustrating for the wife who, as we have learned in Part 2, is generally slower to get sexually aroused.

In women, masturbation often has the opposite effect. Most females masturbate by rubbing or massaging the clitoris. And this little structure is hard to locate, especially by an amateur lover on the honeymoon. As a result a woman who has trained herself to be aroused by clitoral touch may take a long time to be aroused by other stimuli, and may feel frustrated or turned off.

♥ Shame and guilt

Feelings of shame and guilt are formidable pleasure-blockers to sexual enjoyment. Christian couples who have been sexually active before marriage, either all the way to sexual intercourse or stopping just short with genital touching or oral sex, often carry the guilt and shame of their perceived failure to remain pure until their marriage. Shame and guilt may also be the result of sexual sins such as using pornography, fantasising about or having premarital sex with someone other than your marital partner.

A woman who feels this way may find that, while she really enjoyed pushing the boundaries of sexual intimacy before marriage, she feels a lack of desire after the wedding. We see this in Jessica's scenario. A man may also experience these same feelings and have problems getting an erection. Or sometimes may get an erection but not feel desire, or may have a problem reaching orgasm.

Some couples like Emily and Zac had sizzling hot sex before marriage. This was fuelled by the excitement and hidden nature of the 'forbidden' pleasure. Now they have the permission to be sexual but the intimacy is no longer exciting. He doesn't have to pursue her any longer. The thrill of the chase is gone. And she, in spite of the sexy lingerie, feels nothing.

What should you do?

Firstly, you will need to accept God's promises of release and redemption from the past. First-century Corinth was a place of licentiousness and sexual liberty. And yet, after listing all the sexual sins and immoralities, Paul assured the Christians that as God's new creation, they were washed, sanctified and justified in the name of the Lord Jesus Christ and by the Spirit of our God (1 Corinthians 6:11). That same promise of leaving the old behind and becoming new applies to us.

As a couple, you need to discuss the issues. This may not be easy, and may not even be possible during your honeymoon. Don't hurry it. Talk about it and let it rest. Practise the sensuality and mindfulness activities we have described in Appendix 2. These will build new patterns of love, sex and sensuality between the two of you in the safe place of your marriage.

Some of these mind blocks and flashbacks will fade naturally as you spend time caring and loving each other, and build fresh memories and patterns of couple intimacy. Sometimes you may need some help. Don't be afraid to ask for assistance. It may be an older couple, your pastor or a counsellor. Don't leave it too long.

4. Once married, sexual intimacy always ends in intercourse

Remember your first date? When holding hands shot a tremor of excitement down your spine and the first kiss sent you spiralling into space? When you sat together for hours and wondered 'how far is too far'? You were aware of the range of sexual activities from holding hands, cuddling, different levels of kissing, and intimate touches of the body, to oral sex and sexual intercourse. But as young unmarried Christians you set the boundaries of permitted sexual activity to be honouring of your partner and yourself. And you refrained from anything that was sexually arousing, keeping well away from sexual intercourse.

Now you are married. Finally sexual intercourse is permissible! And that becomes the goal.

All the other things you both loved doing—touching, kisses and cuddles which you really enjoyed for the buzz they gave you—now become just the appetiser. You have waited a long time to move from entree to main course. And the main course better be good! And it better stay good for as long as you are a couple. So, instead of being fun, sexual activity becomes a performance, every encounter a gourmet meal, with the anxiety that goes with it and the disappointment when you feel it is less than an award-winner.

What should you do?

Enjoy all aspects of lovemaking. Remind each other of what activities turned you on before marriage. Discuss the boundaries you set to sexual intimacy. Talk over how hard it was to keep the boundaries. Now lovingly and gently cross each of these boundaries together. Remember to laugh and have fun.

Your bodies belong to each other (1 Corinthians 7:2–6). Enjoy the process. These are the first steps on the journey of a lifetime of good sex.

5. Hot love lasts—forever

Jessica and John in the scenario above are typical of a couple who are disappointed that they are no longer hot for each other. It's been only two months, but Jessica feels a lack of interest, desire or libido. And John? Well he wants the physical thrill to go on forever. Emily and Zac are similar. But for them the disappointment starts on the wedding night.

Whatever has happened?

There are a number of reasons why reality may not live up to people's expectations. Some of these we have already discussed, but there are other sexpectations of which couples need to be aware.

♥ Unmatched perceptions

When a couple are dating, the man is constantly making a special attempt to woo his chosen mate. In the dopamine-driven frenzy, he will do anything to win the reward of intimacy with his chosen one. He pursues her, dresses to please, bulks up at the gym—even wears her favourite aftershave. And she likewise spends time and money on her clothes, her make-up and her shoes. They go to fun places and do exciting things that push their norepinephrine and dopamine levels through the roof. They are in the high-tension romance phase.

But now they are married; he has won the prize and no longer needs to pursue her. He is tired, busy. He works overtime, saves money for a home and the planned baby. And she doesn't feel she needs to spend time on dressing up for him. Why bother?

She misses her 'knight in shining armour' who swept her off her feet. He longs for the princess who fascinated him. So desire shrivels and dies for one or both. And sex becomes mundane and a chore.

♥ A move from passionate to 'passional' love

Couples need to recognise that the crazy passion of romantic love or *limerance* lasts months or, at the most, a little over a year. Once the anxiety of uncertainty is resolved by the commitment of marriage, the initial phase of euphoria, excitement and stress evolves into a phase of 'passional love'.[55] This is dominated by feelings of safety, calm and balance. In this second phase, passion occurs in bursts, whereas intimacy and commitment continue to increase steadily. The stress of wooing and pursuing the mate is decreased. In this stage other hormones go up in the brain. Levels of oxytocin and vasopressin, called 'cuddle hormones', increase.

As a couple, you need to acknowledge this change in emotions, and work through to the more stable phase of

55   de Boer, A, van Buel, EM, Ter Horst, GJ 2012, 'Love is more than just a kiss: A neurobiological perspective on love and affection', *Neuroscience*, 201, pp. 114–124.

bonding and attachment. To do otherwise and expect to live in a desire-filled orgasmic haze for all your married life is to invite disappointment and start a downward spiral in your sex life.

These are just a few sexpectations we see in the honeymoon period. You may have others. If you do, then remember that marriage is God's instrument for uniting man and woman into an integrated whole—a shaping of two into one. So, chill. You have plenty of time to shape your intimacy into a lifetime of good sex. And remember, it is OK to ask for help.

Honeymoon to God's glory

We have discussed how the engagement period was a time of training in faithfulness. By that same token, the honeymoon and the early romantic love phase of marriage is the launching pad for growth in godliness. So hang in there if things get rough, and rejoice when all goes well.

Remember, God wants the best for you. As the psalmist says:

For the LORD God is a sun and shield; the LORD bestows favour and honour; no good thing does he withhold from those whose walk is blameless. Lord Almighty, blessed is the one who trusts in you. (Psalm 84:11–12)

Your marriage will be a spice garden of sanctification. To the world, your relationship as man and wife will be an example of Christ and his Church (Ephesians 5).

In the husband's single-minded sacrificial care and the wife's loving submission, Christ's faithfulness and love will be mirrored to the world.

In the mutual grace between husband and wife who

continue to forgive each other (Matthew 18:21–22) and build each other up (1 Thessalonians 5:9–12), the world will see an image of Christ's redemptive grace.

Take-away messages

- Honeymoon sex rarely, if ever, lives up to our expectations.
- It's important to take it slow; mutual exploration and sensuality is far more important and satisfying than instant sexual intercourse. Be patient.
- Don't panic if things go amiss. Enjoy the honeymoon. If the problems persist, ask for help when you get back home.
- The honeymoon is the launching pad for a lifetime of loving. Accept and celebrate it as a gift from a good and gracious God.

Chapter 7
Marriage: spiced-up sanctification

The girls meet regularly for a chat and a cappuccino. They graduated from university eight years ago and are all married now.

Tara and Jenny married their high school sweethearts when still at university. Jenny is now a stay-at-home mum with little kids. Tara helps her husband Roger run a highly successful IT company. Indrani did the right thing by her Indian family and agreed to an arranged marriage soon after graduation to a boy she had met just twice before the wedding day. She works part-time, fortunate to have her mother-in-law as live-in carer to her two daughters.

Kate and Charmaine had concentrated on their careers as investment banker and paediatrician respectively, their sworn singleness breached only recently. They are the newlyweds, less than two years married and without kids.

The conversation usually revolves around clothes, make-up, dieting and reminiscence about the good times at university. Sometimes the conversation strays into mundane areas, such as problems with purchasing a home and financing that ideal holiday.

Today their talk somehow ends up on the topic of sex ...

'It's all Alan's got on his mind', Jenny moans. 'He'd be happy to go at it every night. Like I need more exercise after putting our three little monsters to bed. It's like—OK, let's get it over with and go to sleep. I do love Alan. But all this sex—I am so over it.'

Indrani rolls her kohl-lined eyes. 'I actually don't mind the sex. It's the pressure thing. We've got to have a son—family honour and all that. So it's by the calendar. And my mother-in-law's got this stuff from home ...'

Charmaine leans over the table. Her wavy blonde hair falls over her face. 'Indian aphrodisiacs? I could use some of those!'

Jenny swings round to face her. 'You too? You were the one who knew all the answers in Sex Ed!'

Charmaine laughs and tosses her hair back over her shoulder. 'No. Not me, darling. It's my dear hubby David. He says he really loves me. And I truly believe him. But in the bedroom ...' She pauses and sends her hand palm down in a diving motion under the table. 'He doesn't always get it happening. And when he does, it's like a wham bam thank you ma'am thing.' She looks at Kate. 'How are things for you and Ian?'

'OK, I guess.' Kate, ever the class clown, mimics a yawn, making the others giggle. 'Sort of like plain vanilla.'

The girls sit for a while, absorbing the shared confidences.

Jenny turns to Tara. 'Hey girl, you've been awfully quiet.' She stops and reaches for her friend's hand, shocked at the tears, the muffled sob. 'No. It's alright. You don't have to say anything.'

'I want to', Tara whispers. 'I don't know what to do. At least I can talk to you guys. I ... I can't trust Roger anymore.'

Kate grabs the table knife. 'Another woman? I'll cut off his ...'

Tara's lips twitch. 'No. Another woman I can fight. He's into pornography. And ... and he wants me to try it too. He wants me to act like some porn star ... use stuff. He says everyone's doing it now.' She smiles wistfully at Jenny. 'All this trying for a baby isn't helping either. I feel like some kind of an automaton, watching the calendar, taking the injections.'

There is silence around the table.

Can you empathise with any of these women? Or with their spouses? Maybe it is low libido and desire? The lack of zing in your relationship? Questions about aphrodisiacs and sex toys? The busy and tiring life-stage of having young kids? Or no kids? Or sadly dealing with infidelity or the scourge of pornography?

Why is it that so many couples, like these girls, feel unhappy and discontented in sexually-unfulfilled marriages? And why does it matter?

Why is sexual intimacy in marriage important?

1. Sex and marriage is the arena where man and woman as a couple fulfil God's commands together

Men and women are equal before God in that they are both God's image bearers. However, we don't have to look in the mirror to know that men and women are intrinsically different, and that this difference goes beyond their physical structure. We function, think and respond differently. Nowhere is this difference more profound than in our sexuality.

These differences are not a problem; they're actually what God intended. In Genesis 1, God created humanity as male and female. Genesis 2 gives us more detail: he made the man Adam, and then made the woman Eve from his rib—the same 'stuff' as Adam, his own 'flesh and bone'—but different from him, not simply the same. That's why she was a 'suitable' helper. The term 'suitable' means someone who 'fits' just right, who 'completes' the other person.[56] He then blessed them and commanded them to fill and rule the earth (Genesis 1:26, 28) or, as Genesis 2 puts it, to work the garden together. Marriage between a man and a woman is supposed to be a delightful coming together, a union of the two in serving God.

We recognise this in the marriage ceremony when we say, 'marriage is the symbol of God's unending love for his people, and of union between Christ and his Church'. Further, 'marriage is a *gift from God* for human wellbeing, and for the *proper expression of natural instincts and affections* with which he has endowed us. It is a *lifelong union* in which a man and a woman are called so to *give themselves in body, mind, and spirit*, and so to respond, that from their union will grow a deepening knowledge and love of each other'.[57]

56   Davidson, RM 2007, *Flame of Yahweh: Sexuality in the Old Testament*, Hendrickson, Peabody, pp.19–21.
Hamilton, VP 1990, *The Book of Genesis*, Eerdmans, Grand Rapids, pp. 177–181.
Wenham, GJ 2002, *Word Biblical Commentary: Genesis 1–15*, Word, Waco, pp. 68–72.
57   Marriage Form 1 (2012), *Common Prayer: Resources for Gospel-shaped Gatherings*, Anglican Press Australia, Sydney, p. 117.

What role does sex play in this?

Sexual intercourse plays an obvious role in procreation. The human genitalia are perfectly complementary—when a man and a woman's genitalia function in a normal, healthy way, they work together to make babies. But that's not all. The act of sexual intimacy between two people establishes a deep brain bond[58] between them. It establishes lifelong union of body, mind and spirit. This brain bonding is God's neurochemical plan to make it easier for his image bearers to follow his commands. Lifelong faithfulness to one sexual partner is healthy and natural; chopping and changing partners is not.

2. Sexual intimacy in marriage turns commitment into brain bonding

When a couple stay together, they move from the crazy romantic love phase through the less crazy 'passional' phase and then into a less emotional but infinitely deeper commitment phase.[59] As man and woman, we are created for long-term relationships and God gives us a brain mechanism for this. This phase of a couple's relationship is characterised by feelings of trust, calm, security, social comfort and emotional union. The neural circuitry of this brain system has been associated primarily with neuropeptides, oxytocin and vasopressin. These 'cuddle hormones' increase with any form of intimacy between the couple. An orgasm sends oxytocin levels through the roof.

58   de Boer, A, van Buel, EM, Ter Horst, GJ 2012, 'Love is more than just a kiss: A neurobiological perspective on love and affection', *Neuroscience*, 201, pp.114–124.
59   Starka, L 2007, 'Endocrine factors of pair bonding', *Prague Medical Report*, 108, 4, pp. 297–305.

This shared intimacy of a long-term union brings lovers closer together, potentially triggering a 'virtuous' cycle: the more you make love, the closer you feel, and the closer you feel, the more you make love. And so on. No wonder the writer of the Proverbs encourages a young man to be not just satisfied but intoxicated.

> Drink water from your own cistern, running water from your own well. Should your springs overflow in the streets, your streams of water in the public squares? Let them be yours alone, never to be shared with strangers. May your fountain be blessed, and may you rejoice in the wife of your youth. A loving doe, a graceful deer—may her breasts satisfy you always, may you ever be intoxicated with her love. (Proverbs 5:15–19)

This is the kind of bond that keeps you together after the young blush of romance described in Song of Songs is past and your body is gravity-challenged. When you and your partner are wrinkled and sagging and the athletic lovemaking of your youth is a distant memory (Ecclesiastes 12), your love for each other and your commitment to your marriage will be stronger than it ever was.

3. Sexual intimacy in a couple relationship counteracts sexual temptation

Look around you. The media, television and the internet offer the seductive messages that an extramarital affair is not just harmless; it could even help a boring marriage. Billboards advertise websites devoted to extramarital liaisons with the advice 'Life is short—have an affair'.

There is pleasure for a season in sexual sin. Sex feels good; that's why we do it. Add to this the thrill of the forbidden, the mindboggling chemical buzz. This is why sexual sin feels terrific ... for a while. We must build up our defences long before the temptation gets close. Glossing over the power of sexual temptation leaves us unprepared for testing times.

In the marriage ceremony, the couple vow that they will 'forsaking all others, love and protect'[60] each other as long as they both live. This protection includes sexual fidelity.

Having sexual intercourse with your spouse doesn't necessarily prevent infidelity. But true intimacy between a husband and wife—where each is sensitive to the other's needs and able to serve the other by word, deed and sexual intimacy—places a fence of trust and mutual encouragement around the marriage bed. In 1 Corinthians 7:5, Paul instructs the married couple to make time for sexual intimacy. Do it, he says, as a safeguard against the temptation to sin.

It doesn't always have to be sexual intercourse. Married couples develop their own love language. This may include regular intercourse, or it may include any other of a range of physical and non-physical sexually intimate activities unique to them. It may be a kiss, a cuddle, sometimes even a look that says 'we are in this together'. Sometimes it could be a little love note in the lunchbox or a gift. Whatever these are, they form the glue that holds the marriage together and protects it against intruders.

60   Marriage Form 1 (2012), *Common Prayer: Resources for Gospel-shaped Gatherings*, Anglican Press Australia, Sydney.

4. Sexual intimacy feels good, and keeps you healthy

Sex makes you feel great. Even a hug increases the levels of oxytocin. Sexual intercourse bathes your brain in oxytocin and the related feel-good chemicals like endorphins and dopamine. Orgasm sends these levels sky-high with frissons of pleasure through your body. Oxytocin also has anxiolytic and stress-reducing effects and induces feelings of trust. Endorphins have a narcotic-like, sedative effect. Dopamine induces the feelings of love for the partner. This euphoria is expressed by the woman and her husband in the Song of Songs. She says, 'My beloved is to me a sachet of myrrh resting between my breasts. My beloved is to me a cluster of henna blossoms from the vineyards of En Gedi' (1:13–14). He responds, 'How much more pleasing is your love than wine, and the fragrance of your perfume more than any spice! Your lips drop sweetness as the honeycomb, my bride; milk and honey are under your tongue' (4:10–11). That sure sounds exciting!

Researchers point out the many health benefits of sexual intimacy[61], especially sexual intercourse. The frequency of sexual intercourse is directly related to how both men and women perceive their mental health. There is also a direct relationship with measures of satisfaction, intimacy, trust, passion and love. Other research suggests a relationship between the frequency of intercourse and improved cardiovascular health and lower blood pressure.[62]

61   Brody, S 2010, 'The relative health benefits of different sexual activities', *Journal of Sexual Medicine*, 7, pp. 1336–1361.
62   Brody, S & Preut, R 2003, 'Vaginal intercourse frequency and heart rate variability', *Journal of Sex and Marital Therapy*, 29, pp. 371–380.

Is there any wonder that the writer of Proverbs recommends that a man drink water from his own cistern, the running water from his own well (5:15). 'Let them be yours alone, never to be shared with strangers' (5:17). Marriage is described as a wonderful relationship in which a man can rejoice in one wife from youth onwards (5:18), always finding her sexually satisfying and captivating (5:19). The mutual commitment encouraged by the Scriptures implies that the wife should also find marriage a wonderful and satisfying relationship (31:10–31).

5. Intimacy in marriage mirrors Christ and the Church

The love relationship between a man and a woman is an illustration of the love relationship within the Trinity, between God and Israel, and between Christ and the Church (Hosea 3:1; Malachi 2:10–16; Ephesians 5:32; John 3:35; John 5:20; John 15:9; John 16:13–15). It is more than the emotional romance of a dopamine high. Rather it is the covenant commitment of faithfulness for life, irrespective of what life throws up at the couple.

God loved Israel in spite of their adulterous behaviour with the idols of other nations, which God likened to prostitutes:

> The Lord said to me, 'Go, show your love to your wife again, though she is loved by another man and is an adulteress. Love her as the Lord loves the Israelites, though they turn to other gods and love the sacred raisin cakes'. (Hosea 3:1)

And he showed this love most of all in Christ, who gave his body to death for us. According to Paul, God has so intimately connected Christ to his people that the Church is Christ's body (Ephesians 5:25–32). This is just like sex binds a man and a woman, body and 'soul', both physically in the act of intercourse, and through the deep connection, the union of life, that long-term sex gives.

So this model of Christ and the Church is both a gift and a calling for marriage. It's a gift in that God has created our bodies in such a way that fulfilling his commands brings us pleasure and satisfaction, both to our bodies and to our affections, our emotions. And it's a calling in that God invites us to decide to shape our married life around the model of Christ and his Church. The cross of Christ is the model for the ultimate one-flesh intimacy between married couples. To be one flesh is to give ourselves up for the other, to care for their comfort and pleasure more than our own. In this, our marriages will be evangelistic: they will display Christ to the world.

Take-away messages

- Sexual intimacy is an important part of the marriage relationship. However it is a part and not the whole.
- Sexual intimacy is not just sexual intercourse. The Song of Songs reminds us that a good sex life comes from focusing on the whole person and not on the body.
- Sexual intimacy is the glue that holds a marriage together and mirrors Christ's cruciform love for his Church.

Chapter 8
Good sex in marriage

Unfortunately, knowing and accepting God's plan for marriage and sex doesn't mean that things work out as we expect. Sometimes our expectations are too high, they are mismatched, or just too hard to achieve. Sometimes illness gets in the way. Or we allow work and the daily grind of home life to take away the gloss. Sometimes children and parenting become an obstacle to intimacy. We are disappointed. We feel sad and let down by our partner. We know we need to do something. But what should we do? And where do we get help?

Let's go back to the women's conversation over coffee at the beginning of Chapter 7 and explore some of the sexual intimacy issues they raised.

1. Lost libido: when one wants sex more (or less) than the other

What is sexual desire?

Sexologists describe sexual desire as 'the presence of sexual thoughts, fantasies and interest in sexual activity'. When the lack of desire leads to severe personal distress or relationship difficulties, it is given the label Hypoactive Sexual Desire Disorder (HSDD).

We have all felt desire for something. By definition and by brain chemistry, this is a hunger, a drive for personal gratification. Desire is about 'me' and what 'I want'. Sexual desire is no different. It's just that the 'need' is for sex. It is also the kick-off point for sexual activity between two people. As we have already discussed, it is a God-given primal urge designed to draw a man and woman together to have sex, both for pleasure and for procreation.

'My spouse wants sex more/less than me' is the most common sexual concern sex therapists see in consultation rooms. Researchers tell us that 27–32% of sexually-active women and 13–17% of men aged 18–59 reported lack of interest in sex over several months or more in the prior year.[63] Frankly, as a sex therapist, I am surprised that the concern isn't universal. Think about it. After all, what is a sexual thought? Surely there are many different ways in which to express interest in sexual activity. As a married couple, we don't always feel hungry at the same time and when we do, it's unlikely that

63   Meana, M 2010, 'Elucidating women's (hetero) sexual desire: Definitional challenges and content expansion', *Journal of Sex Research*, 47, 2–3, pp. 104–122.

we'll want the identical menu item in the same portion size. The same would hold true if we were to think of what we like to read, watch on television or do in our recreational time. Why should we think that it would be different when it comes to sex?

Look at the biology: males have about ten times as much testosterone (the desire hormone) coursing through their bloodstream as women. So, in general, men have a jump-start on desire. Secondly, men are also more turned on when they see, hear and/or smell something. Women take longer. As we discussed in Part 2, women are like a slow-cooking crockpot to the male quick heat-up microwave desire. We see this quick turn-on and easily-satisfied response in Alan and Jenny's lovemaking.

Not only are males and females different, but every person is unique. You may be on the lower end of the scale in terms of sexual thoughts, fantasy and interest, but have a very satisfying sex life. Two thirds of women who say that they desire sex less than once a week, actually engage in sex more often than that and are sexually satisfied and happy with the relationship.[64] This tells us that many women experience a satisfying sexual life without the outright desire for sexual activity. This is different in men. In the male sexual response, sexual desire is generally a necessary prequel to erections. This is true even when using medication for erection problems. It is no surprise that men and women find it difficult to understand each other's desire patterns.

64   Brotto, LA, Bitzer, J, Laan, E, Leiblum, S & Luria, M 2010, 'Women's sexual desire and arousal disorders', *Journal of Sexual Medicine*, 7, pp. 586–614.

Further, sexual desire is not solely a biological act. Every one of us has built up a script of what turns us on and what turns us off. We become very specific in the stimuli that turn on our desire. It's not just perfume, but Chanel No.5; not just lipstick but that particular shade of hot pink. A person might be really turned on by music—not just music in general, but classical music and, more specifically, Mozart, and especially the horn concertos. Another finds that music does nothing for him or her. Rather it's a particular gesture, or being touched in a certain way or on a particular part of the body. Your culture, religious and ethnic background, sexual experiences and psychological development from childhood, working with your biological make-up, all influence your sexual desire.[65] This in turn affects how you respond sexually once you get started on your sexual journey. Each person has their own stimulus for this wonderful God-given sexual appetite, a brain programming that begins from childhood.

Is it any wonder that the Bible is clear on the importance of the impressionable years of childhood? In Deuteronomy 11:18–20, the onus is clearly on the parents to nurture good thinking in their children. Parents are to talk to their children about God's message at all times: 'when you sit at home and when you walk along the road, when you lie down and when you get up'. Maybe today's equivalent would be when driving children to school, over family meals and relaxing around a video or television show.

65   Levine, S 2003, 'The nature of sexual desire: A clinician's perspective', *Archives of Sexual Behaviour*, 32, pp. 279–285.

In Proverbs 1:8–10, the writer warns the son against following foolish paths, advising him to listen to his father's instruction and not forsake his mother's teaching.

If you have been raised in a family where sex was a taboo topic and all you ever heard was 'don't do it', then your brain may be wired to see sex as dirty and forbidden. You will probably have abstained from sexual intimacy before marriage not only because you wanted to stay pure, but because it wasn't something you viewed as nice. You may have even felt guilty about the sexual thrill you felt when your fiancée or fiancé touched you. Or, as part of an engaged couple, you may have pushed the boundary of physical intimacy and then felt sick and ashamed of what you did.

If this is you, you need to understand and accept that sex is a good gift created by God to be enjoyed in marriage (Genesis 2:22–25; Song of Songs). It is a one-flesh naked and no-shame activity of love and bonding. All things are created for and by God (Colossians 1:16). And we can be very certain that nothing God created is evil in itself (1 Timothy 4:4). Whatever the messages of your childhood may have been, you can accept the gift of sex in the marriage relationship as a wonderful and pleasurable gift from God, and give him thanks for it.

The brain programming doesn't stop after the teenage years. Sex science tells us that your brain absorbs and is influenced by what you do and see, even as an adult. If you feed it high-quality information in the form of healthy relationships and pure thoughts towards others, both males and females, you'll be rewarded with wholesome and healthy sexual feelings. On the other hand, if you feed your mind with impure thoughts like the unwholesome images and non-relational selfish sex of pornography, you'll find that your sexual thoughts, fantasies and activities will reflect these.

The Apostle Paul knew something about this brain programming when he instructed the Philippians to beware of what they fed their mind (Philippians 4:8). He went into detail on the characteristics of the content. Today, as it was 2000 years ago, we need to feed our brains with 'whatever is true, whatever is noble, whatever is right, whatever is pure, whatever is lovely, whatever is admirable—if anything is excellent or praiseworthy'.

Sexual desire is a brain thing. Your personal response at the specific moment of sexual intimacy is the outcome of your emotional brain juggling all the immediate sensory input of touch, sound and everything else, and filtering it through the mesh of learned and prewired memories and responses.

Is it any wonder that the couples in our scenarios struggle to match up their wants and needs for sexual intimacy? In the case of Jenny and Alan, it seems to be Jenny with the low libido, while in Charmaine and David's relationship, it's David. It sounds like Kate and her husband have slipped into a boring pattern of lovemaking. And in Tara's marriage we see the outcome of a compulsive use of pornography, as well as the pressure couples feel when trying to get pregnant.

Let's explore some possible reasons for these mismatches in desire and what these couples could do to kick start their libido. We will explore here the most common causes for discrepancies in sexual desire: ignorance of sexual arousal patterns and brain blockers to desire.

Ignorance of male and female sexual arousal patterns

Even in this sexually-enlightened age, many married men and women struggle with a poor understanding of their own body and that of their partner.

The structure of the genitals and the male and female sexual response has been discussed in Part 2. If you skipped those chapters, go back and read them now.

We know that the male and female bodies are very similar, except for their reproductive and genital organs and the secondary sexual characteristics like body hair and breasts. What most don't realise is that the sexual response in a man and a woman is also different. In short, a man is generally easily aroused and moves relatively quickly through arousal to orgasm. The woman, however, may go into sexual intercourse feeling sexually neutral—not desiring sex, but accepting her husband's advances for love and intimacy. But then, as her husband romances her, an amazing thing happens. She finds that she is sexually aroused and her desire increases. And she enjoys the experience, whether or not she climaxes in an orgasm.

But, if sexual activity is about romancing and being romanced, a couple needs to know each other's preferences. Where and how does she like to be touched? What sexual positions would he like to explore?

How do a couple communicate their personal likes and dislikes when it comes to touching, kissing and being sexually aroused? This is a difficult conversation at many levels. Firstly, most of us are socialised not to talk openly about what are our 'private parts'. So even in the naked and no-shame environment of the marriage bed, this conversation can be embarrassing. Secondly, most of us aren't sure what turns us on, much less what turns on our spouse. We draw on what we have in our brain scripts: books, television shows and, sadly, in some cases pornography. And most times neither our own body nor that of our spouse is anything like what we have in our minds. How can we tell our lover what we like, when we really don't know ourselves?

Finally, many men think they are supposed to know how to make love—that it is some form of instinctive knowledge, while actually it is scripting from what they have learned and experienced growing up. They don't ask their spouse, 'Is this good for you?' but feel rejected and hurt when their spouse is not turned on. The wife is confused. She too has expected him to know what to do to turn her on sexually. They feel stuck, neither knowing how to proceed. So, lovemaking becomes some sort of obligatory activity, rather than the joyful coming together that God meant it to be.

Communicating about sexual preferences is necessary for good sex. It can also be enlightening and great fun. In therapy, I use a form titled 'How do I love thee?' to stimulate conversation on lovemaking (Appendix 3). You may find this a useful starting point for your own conversation on personal preferences. In this activity, you first reflect on what you enjoy and what you 'think' your spouse likes. You then share this with him or her. Make time to do it. Be prepared to be surprised, even if you have been married for a while.

The other activity I recommend is more practical and hands-on. Here the exploration goes beyond talking to slow and gentle, other-focused sensuality activities (Appendix 2). Couples get to know each other's bodies and enjoy learning what turns the other on. It is done slowly and leisurely.

Husband and wife explore the senses in each other. The activities are adapted from what sexologists call 'sensate focus exercises'[66] and is grounded on biblical principles of good sex. This takes the intimacy encounter into and beyond conversation to behaviour. Through these you will reframe your sexual intimacy. In the process you will find that your relationship as a whole will become infinitely richer.

You may find that doing these exercises as a couple increases your sexual desire and improves your lovemaking. However, sometimes sexual behaviour patterns and the underlying causes are too ingrained to change with these couple activities alone. If this is the case you may need help. Talk to an older, wiser Christian couple. And if need be, don't be ashamed to contact a counsellor or therapist.

Let's now elaborate on some of these blocks to sexual desire.

Brain blockers to desire

Sometimes, learning to communicate and obediently follow sensuality exercises is not enough. This is due to obstacles to intimacy that have built up over time, and an attempt to talk or be intimate falls over at the first hurdle. It may even bring up deep hurts and prejudices.

We call these 'brain blockers'.

Think back to the time when you were in that crazy romantic love phase, even before you were married and had sexual intercourse. Your partner occupied the whole of your

---

66   Originally developed by Masters, W & Johnson, V 1970, *Human sexual inadequacy*, Ishi Press International, USA.

mind when you were together. There was so much to explore, to experiment with and find out.

And then, when newly married, you had only one thought: giving and getting pleasure. You longed to know and be known by your partner. You were intimately in the moment.

But things have changed. You are older and have a history together. It's a terrain well-travelled and you *think you know* what pleases him or her. You're on cruise control on a totally predictable road. You leave lovemaking until late in the night when you are both exhausted. You make an attempt to concentrate, but your mind wanders. The 'to-do' externalities of daily living intrude: the reports you have to write, the washing that still needs doing. Or maybe it's couple issues: 'She doesn't understand me.' 'He hurt me by what he did (or didn't do).' 'He spends too much time with his friends.' 'She gossips.' Or maybe even 'he didn't do the dishes'. You just want to get the intercourse over with and go to sleep. You can empathise with Jenny!

There are the expectations of perfect performance as well. This is often confounded by the memory of an occasion (or more) when you/your husband couldn't get it up, come at the right time, or come at all. This is so common in couples that sex therapists give it a name: 'performance anxiety'. It may be that this is what's happening for David and Charmaine.

The hardest brain blockers to overcome are personal ones. Sometimes these are body image issues. You don't feel attractive enough, or you think your body is saggy or stretched after the baby. Maybe when you were young, your friends teased you about your genitals. Now you feel inadequate. Sometimes there are intrusive feelings of guilt and shame over past sexual experiences, pornography or the use of prostitutes. At worst there are painful memories of growing up, sadness and/or sexual abuse.

How do you overcome brain blockers?

Removal of brain blockers needs immediate and long-term actions.

Firstly, couples with these issues need to refocus on their intimacy as a couple. They need to schedule time to make love. Yes, *schedule*. Let me enlighten you: complete spontaneity in lovemaking happens only very occasionally. Constant spontaneous lovemaking, somewhat like simultaneous orgasms, is a myth— nice but rare and unnecessary. Making time for lovemaking is not always easy. And sadly 'we don't have time' becomes an excuse that really means 'I don't want to put the energy into working on the problem'. Look at the couples in our vignettes. Jenny says she is 'so over sex'. What she really means is that she wants her husband to understand the pressures of home and three children. She would probably find his help in getting the kids ready and put to bed a great prequel to lovemaking. But she never tells him. Instead she assumes that he should know what she wants. He doesn't. And so nothing changes.

Having made a time in their life for lovemaking, couples need to practise staying in the moment as they make love. Staying in the moment requires developing a thinking process that shuts out all the intrusive thoughts and concentrates on the person you are with. Concentrating on his or her body and yours—how it feels for both of you—in pleasuring and being pleasured. This involves looking, enjoying and learning to laugh together. Persevere and discuss the good and bad feelings in the open environment of vulnerability and trust.

This is what other-focused mindful loving looks like.[67] Couples need to set aside special time for it. Put in the effort. It won't happen overnight. Take stops along the way to evaluate where you are. If you stick with it as a couple, you will enjoy the journey as well as the destination.

Within the marriage commitment of being naked and no-shame with one another, all the joys of being lovers come together. It is here that you realise the freedom to express those joys without restraint, knowing that the marriage bond seals your love in a lifetime commitment to each other. The married lovers in Song of Songs accomplished this. The bold but tender scenes point to a major difference between the world's concept of love and what was created and endorsed by God. In the former case the focus is on self-gratification. In the latter, the emphasis is on the wellbeing of the loved one and the extolling of his or her virtues. This is true sensuality, given and received.

The lovers in the Song of Songs took it slow. You can, too.

In the longer term, however, couples must work towards resolving their brain blockers. Sometimes all it needs is time for the couple to talk it over. This request for the conversation could take the form of an email or letter at the beginning. Be careful if you choose to go with the written format. I would recommend it be a note that states clearly how *you* feel, and goes on to ask your spouse to make time to talk. Do not be critical or judgemental when writing or emailing. This is only a starting point. It must graduate to a face-to-face discussion.

At other times the interpersonal issues are deep-seated

67   See Appendix 2 for a step-by-step guide to sensual loving.

and painful. Pornography, infidelity and a history of abuse would fit into this 'hard to resolve' basket. These issues require repentance and forgiveness on one or both sides of the partnership. Remember, we worship a God who forgives our deepest and most devious faults (Romans 3:23–24). It is his grace, offered freely, that heals us. We need to turn this grace and forgiveness outwards to our spouse.

This can be enormously difficult. The hurts that separate us can be firmly established and very real. And yet, we are called to love as Christ loves and forgive as he does. Jesus said that we were to forgive a brother (or sister) 77 times seven (Matthew 18:21–22). How much more should we forgive the man or woman we are committed to for life?

Sometimes, personal repentance and forgiveness by the spouse may suffice. In other couples, counselling may be needed. In more complicated situations, there may be a physical concern that needs investigation (for example, premature ejaculation or erectile dysfunction in the male or vaginismus in the female). This will need external help. Your general practitioner or a therapist will be able to advise you.

The issues may be so deep-seated that face-to-face discussion may be difficult, even impossible, for some couples. As members of a family in the Church, there is nothing shameful about discussing your concerns in a respectful way with other trusted couples. This sharing must, of course, be agreeable to both husband and wife.

The sexual health of couples is important to the family of the Church. Wisdom from the community can be supportive, and can bring a new vision to the issue.

Remember that sexual desire in marriage is not a solo

activity. It is necessarily other-focused. It looks to please and pleasure rather than seek self-gratification.

This takes us to the next concern. How do you bring more excitement into your lovemaking?

2. Bringing the zing back into marriage

Maybe, like Kate, your sex life as a couple has gone from an exciting multi-flavoured sundae ice-cream to plain vanilla. Or maybe it was always plain vanilla, and you have looked at the many sexual activities portrayed in the media and internet and wondered if some of these might add some spice and exoticism to your love-life. You listen to friends talk about all that they do and wonder how it would be to try an aphrodisiac or a sex toy, watch a sex video, or at least bring some new activity or position to your lovemaking.

Should you do it?

As a Christian, is there a right and wrong approach to sex and lovemaking in marriage? One that is godly? Who do you approach with these questions? Or is anything OK between the two of you?

Let's look again at the general principles. Firstly, sex is good. It is a gift from God to us. He created us as man and woman with exquisitely matched genitalia and desire for each other. In our coming together we celebrate and honour that unique one-flesh relationship, one that mirrors, in a small way, Christ's relationship with the Church (Ephesians 5:25–33).

How should this affect our sexual behaviour?

It means that we, as husband and wife, are made as man and woman before Christ. Our sexual activity, like all other aspects of our relationship, should honour the other. Any activity should ultimately strengthen our marriage such that it is a blessing to the larger community of the Church, and thereby bring glory to God. So, we never force or coerce our spouse. Rather, we seek always to please, even if it means forgoing something we like.

Secondly, we need to recognise that sexual activity is more—much more—than sexual intercourse. It is anything that involves you in a sexual act either by yourself or with another person. So, masturbation is a solo sexual activity, as is fantasy. Watching pornography, with the lustful thoughts that accompany it, is sex. Kissing, snogging, cuddling, petting, genital touching, fingering, oral sex, anal sex and intercourse are all sexual activities. (You may be able to think of others.) Even a tasteless sexualised joke or the lyrics of rap songs meant to arouse and titillate can be a sexual activity in the mind of the person verbalising it, and in the minds of the audience. As Christians we need to recognise how far the wonderful gift of sex has been twisted by Satan. It is then that we can gird our hearts and brains to maintain the sexual purity in our lives. Remember, sexual purity is important to God (Ephesians 5:2–4).

Given this context, what can a Christian couple do to bring the zing, sizzle or fire back to their sex life? Is it OK to try something new? And if so, what?

Doing something different and new will bring excitement to your relationship. It pushes up the chemical norepinephrine in the brain. It increases dopamine levels; it's exhilarating and brings the crazy romantic rush that seemed long gone back into your life as a couple.

This is good. But remember that, as husband and wife,

what will keep you bonded and together for life will not be the momentary thrill of a novel sex act. It will be the deeply committed, other-focused loving of your covenant marriage relationship.

You see, what you do with your bodies and minds as husband and wife matters deeply to God. Like our society today, the people of Corinth were into all sorts of variant sexual activity. And Paul wrote to them saying:

> 'I have the right to do anything', you say—but not everything is beneficial. 'I have the right to do anything' —but I will not be mastered by anything. You say, 'Food for the stomach and the stomach for food, and God will destroy them both'. The body, however, is not meant for sexual immorality but for the Lord, and the Lord for the body. (1 Corinthians 6:12–13)

When you as a couple consider branching out into some novel activity, we suggest the following questions as principles to your decision-making. Answer these questions individually and then discuss them as a couple.

1. Does this activity **honour** my spouse and our marriage? Am I seeing and treating him or her as I would my own body? Or does it degrade him or her to being an object of my personal pleasure and sexual gratification?
2. Does this activity have the **potential to harm** my spouse either physically or emotionally?
3. Does this activity build up my spouse and our marriage relationship? Is it an activity you would feel **comfortable** speaking about with other couples in church? I am not recommending that you keep a diary of what you do as a

couple and take it to the next Bible study meeting! Rather, I am asking you to run the specific sexual activity through the filter of God's pattern for good sex. Any activity that you feel uncomfortable or in any way embarrassed or queasy about is probably not a wise practice.

We will explore some common sexual activities with these principles in mind.

♥ Anal sex

We have listed kissing, snogging, cuddling, petting, genital touching, fingering, oral sex, anal sex and intercourse all as sexual activities between a couple.

Would any of these fail to pass the three-stage test?

Most of them would pass the test. We say 'most' because anal sex is the one that fails all three.

Anal sex means sexual activity involving the bottom—in particular the type of intercourse in which the penis goes into the anus. It's also referred to as 'rectal sex'. It was originally thought that this was an activity that was practised only by gay men. We now know that this is not the case. Although it is difficult to know the exact proportion, it is estimated that about a third of heterosexual couples have tried anal sex at some time in their relationship.[68]

While the term is generally used to mean penis in anus, there are a number of other sexual activities that involve the anus. These include activities like putting a finger into the

---

68 McBride, KR & Fortenberry, JD 2010, 'Heterosexual anal sexuality and anal sex behaviors: A review', *Journal of Sex Research*, 47:2–3, pp. 123–136.

partner's bottom, insertion of 'butt plugs' (which are sex toys that dilate the anal opening and create a sensation of fullness), and 'rimming' (which is oral–anal contact).

Anal sexual activities carry very real dangers. The lining of the anus and lower rectum is not suited for the abrasion and pressure of the entry of a penis or any other object. It is easily torn on penetration. Once torn, the passage of faeces means it takes time to heal and may result in infection and pain.

Among women and adolescents, heterosexual anal sex is a factor in transmission of several sexually transmitted infections (STIs), including Human Immunodeficiency Virus (HIV). There is also emerging evidence that anal sex leads to Human Papillomavirus (HPV) infection and consequential anal cancer.[69] The likelihood of infection is increased by the fact that many couples do not use a condom when having anal sex, the rationale probably being that there is no danger of pregnancy.

Sex scientists believe that the increased interest in heterosexual anal sex is driven by easy access to pornography. Girls report being pressured or coerced by their male partners to have anal sex when they refuse penis-in-vagina sexual intercourse. The use of sex toys such as butt plugs and vibrators further objectify the women who receive them anally.

The Bible does not specifically forbid anal sex. However, I would suggest that apart from the obvious physical dangers discussed above, the practice is neither honouring of the woman and the sexuality of marriage, nor edifying to the couple relationship. It is an act best avoided.

69   ibid.

♥ Oral sex

Another activity sex therapists are asked about is oral sex. Oral sex is the activity where one person stimulates the genitals of the other orally. It can involve kissing, licking or sucking. The term *cunnilingus* (oral vaginal contact) is used when a man stimulates a woman with his mouth or tongue. *Fellatio* (oral penile contact) is used for stimulation of a man's penis by his partner's mouth or tongue.

Couples use oral sex both as an adjunct to sexual intercourse and as a replacement for it when they don't want a pregnancy and are not using contraception. It is an act of close and intense intimacy, and one that both partners need to discuss and be comfortable giving and receiving. Many women who find it difficult to have an orgasm with sexual intercourse find oral sex, with the direct stimulation of the clitoris, intensely pleasurable and often orgasmic.

Some men and women dislike oral sex. This is tied in with their attitudes to sex and knowledge of the genitals. Some believe that the genitals are dirty and oral sex will cause bugs to pass from the receiver to the giver. This can happen, but only if the receiver has a sexually transmitted infection. Without this, infections do not occur. The oral cavity actually has more bugs than the vagina or penis. Others see oral sex as something only sex workers practise. This too is untrue.

So, the decision whether to include oral sex in your sexual activity repertoire is something that you as a couple need to discuss and agree on.

♥ Masturbation

What about masturbation? Does masturbation have a place in married sex?

Masturbation as a sexual activity as a couple carries nuances of context and intention. Masturbation by definition is solo self-stimulation for the precise purpose of sexual arousal and pleasure. We have discussed the pitfalls of masturbation as a sexual practice in an earlier chapter. However, there are some contexts for married couples where masturbation may be an acceptable activity. This is where a couple are separated for long periods of time (for example, one spouse being deployed overseas), or when illness makes sexual intimacy unfeasible (for example, after surgery or in some forms of disability). In these situations the masturbation is a tension release and the fantasies are built around the spouse. We would suggest that such activity within this context passes the three-point test.

Masturbation while being married is unhealthy when the context becomes one of selfish self-gratification. Here, one spouse stimulates him or herself to orgasm rather than sharing their body and arousal with their partner. This easily escalates to lust, with sinful fantasies involving other people.

Mutual genital touching, where one spouse stimulates the genitals of the other as part of sex play, is not masturbation (although it is sometimes erroneously given the name 'mutual masturbation').

♥ Adjuncts to sexual activity—sex toys

Sex toys, aphrodisiacs and erotica—do they contribute to sexual intimacy in marriage? Are they acceptable? Do they pass the three-point test? Shops for sex toys or sex aids, as some adult retailers like to call them, provide a plethora of objects in a variety of materials, textures and colours. The most common and best known are the penis substitute devices known as 'dildos'. Some are flexible and malleable; others are battery-operated to vibrate (thus the name 'vibrators'), light up and even play music. The newer ones are electronic and come with a remote control. All of them do one thing: they aim to increase arousal, and most often mimic sexual activity, especially intercourse. The problem with using a dildo is that they are designed to bring about quick arousal by intense stimulation. In a sexually normal couple, the use of a vibrating penis substitute could set up an expectation of a quick orgasmic release, which would be difficult if not impossible to mimic in male–female sexual intercourse. Some couples use dildos as an occasional fun addition to their sexual repertoire. This is a personal choice. But regular use could result in unrealistic expectations and emotional and relational problems.

There are other sex toys which are adjuncts to light sexual play. These may grade a tick for all three categories. These are the kind that can often be found in novelty shops. An example is sex dice. Here one die has the names of body parts and the other the actions that can be done. If both partners agree on using these, they are a fun and safe way to introduce novelty and variety. The chatting that is required in playing with the dice provides an opening to discuss preferences for specific sexual activities. It is the kind of sex toy that a couple can enjoy. These can even be a fun topic for a chat with other Christian friends. There are other toys, such as board games like Monogamy®, Table Topics® and Food for Thought Couples' Edition® that fit into this category.

Sexy lingerie sold in adult retail stores often mimics that worn by porn stars. Pretty (and less expensive) lingerie available from the regular department store you shop in would be just as functional in lovemaking.

There are other sex toys that are a definite no-no. These include those that mimic bondage and punishment (handcuffs or whips), costumes that caricature a fantasy lover (schoolgirl, nurse, pirate, etc. which are pornography role-play tools and not healthy practice), and other invasive sex tools that have the potential to injure the anus or vagina.

♥ Aphrodisiacs, love potions and medications

The Bible doesn't forbid the use of something to boost sex drive. In fact, it is suggested that the mandrake plant bartered between Leah and Rachel for the sexual favours of their husband Jacob (Genesis 30:14–15) was both an aphrodisiac and a hallucinogen. We also come across the aphrodisiac use of the mandrake and pomegranates in the Song of Songs (7:12–13). Today, we have more than the mandrake and pomegranate available to us.

There are three categories of substances that are used to 'boost sex life'.

The first is where a sexual concern has an underlying physical cause and a doctor determines that a medication would assist sexual function. These are not strictly aphrodisiacs; they are medications. This category includes hormone replacement therapy and the class of what are called PDE5 inhibitor drugs for male erection problems. Recently, a combination of testosterone and PDE5 inhibitor-type medication[70] has been trialled for women with decreased libido. These medications

---

70   Bergner, D 2013, 'Unexcited? There may be a pill for that', *The New York Times Magazine*, viewed June 15 2013, <http://www.nytimes.com/2013/05/26/magazine/unexcited-there-may-be-a-pill-for-that.html?pagewanted=all&_r=0>.

are to be used only under a doctor's advice. Neither hormones (such as testosterone) nor erectile function drugs (such as Viagra, Cialis and Levitra) should ever be taken to enhance desire or sexual function without medical advice. They are not party drugs.

The second category is foods that are said to increase libido and arousal, and are therefore classed as aphrodisiacs. These include foods that have visual similarity to an aroused penis or have been attributed aphrodisiac uses by the virtue of tradition. These include fruits like bananas, pomegranates, strawberries and avocados, as well as chocolate, honey, ginger and oysters. Even the capsaicin in red chillies has been attributed with aphrodisiac properties, as have the antioxidants in black tea. Foods like these are harmless, if unproven, for their aphrodisiac characteristics. So try them if you like. If something turns you on sexually, that's because your main sex organ is between your ears and not between your legs! It's the thought that something is an aphrodisiac that is likely to make it so. The stuff that Indrani's mother-in-law brought from India probably fits into this category.

The third category of substances includes those touted, mostly on the internet, as libido-boosting drugs and recreational drugs marketed as aphrodisiacs. These libido boosters vary from the oldest and totally ineffective, such as Rhino's horn (for which poachers killed the magnificent beasts) and deer antlers (because they look like an erect penis), to chemicals such as ginseng and yohimbe which are herbal remedies that can have side effects, especially if a person is taking other medications. Another substance called Spanish fly (a beetle) is a definite no-no. It causes burning and irritation of the urethra.

Recreational drugs such as methamphetamine (Meth), cocaine, ecstasy (MDMA-4-methylenedioxy-methamphetamine), marijuana (THC) and of course alcohol are all attributed with sex and libido-boosting properties. These drugs work by changing the brain's chemical balance and, while they seemingly boost sexual desire, they actually inhibit conscious decision-making and perception. They are dangerous because they increase sexual risk-taking behaviour, and can cause habituation and, finally, drug addiction. We would definitely not recommend their use in couple sexual activity.

So if, as a couple, you would like to try crystallised ginger and chilli chocolate or a good cup of Sri Lankan tea, go ahead; add it to the supper menu. However the other aphrodisiacs, love potions and medications may be physically or psychologically harmful, and are definitely not honouring and edifying.

The best aphrodisiac ever created is love. Take time to find out what your spouse enjoys. Go back to your love story. What did you do in those early dopamine-filled moments? What sent your norepinephrine surging? These will give you a high that no aphrodisiac ever can.

♥ Erotic videos as sex stimulants

Some time ago, the use of erotic and how-to or pseudo-educational videos was accepted as part of sex and relationships therapy. Now, this is not a common practice. We recognise that many of these videos are in fact 'soft' pornography. Most have men and women with perfectly shaped, buffed bodies demonstrating sexual positions and acts, sometimes individually as in self-masturbation, and at other times in couple sexual activity.

What are the dangers?

The actors in these videos are just that—actors. Their loving looks and gasps of pleasure are performance. It presents us with fantasy sex. The acts and positions may not be to the liking or preference of one or both of the partners watching the video. It leads to unreal expectations (that is, 'we have to do this or that').

Although these videos are (generally) fairly standard in terms of sexual activity, they are still pornographic in nature. Therefore these videos could set a person who already has a tendency towards porn use, on the slippery slope of increasing use, and with it will come all the personal and relational destructive effects.

This takes us to the next area of pornography in marriage.

3. When pornography use enters a marriage

Never use pornography as a sexual aid to increase sexual desire and performance. It is a dangerous and destructive practice.[71] Pornography use destroys marital trust and intimacy. It is diametrically removed from a 'one-flesh, naked and no-shame' (Genesis 2:25) relationship. Unfortunately in our sexualised, technology-driven society, it is now one of the most common concerns therapists see in couple therapy.

In a 1995 interview, the late Princess Diana said, 'There were three of us in this marriage, so it was a bit crowded'.[72] In many marriages today, pornography is that third person. It

71   An excellent book on pornography and its effects is that written by William Struthers, 2009 *Wired for Intimacy: How Pornography Hijacks the Male Brain*, InterVarsity Press, USA.
72   Transcript 'The Panorama interview', BBC, viewed June 10 2013, <http://www.bbc.co.uk/news/special/politics97/diana/panorama.html>.

crowds out intimacy, sets unrealistic expectations, and leads to sexual dysfunction and infidelity.

Why is pornography particularly problematic for Christians?

Nothing in the Church is more taboo than sexual sin. Indeed, as we have discussed, the hallmark of Christian virtue is sexual purity. The Bible repeatedly exhorts us to abstain from sexual immorality and to pursue purity (1 Thessalonians 4:5; 2 Timothy 2:22; 1 Peter 1:14; 2:11; 1 John 2:16). Jesus recommended radical removal of the source of temptation (Matthew 5:27–30). Christians, as believers of God's word, set a high biblical standard of sexual purity and condemn sexual sins. It is right that we do so.

Unfortunately, this sometimes leads to sexuality in itself being seen as either forbidden or 'naughty'. Sexual activity outside the 'permitted' marriage relationship becomes an exciting taboo activity. The Apostle Paul recognised the attraction of such forbidden activities (Romans 5:20; Romans 7:21–24).

A result of this taboo is that sexual sins, both premarital and extramarital, are kept secret in the church environment, and people continue to carry an increasingly heavy burden of shame and guilt. This secrecy is hard to maintain when the specific sin involves premarital sex or an affair. Eventually someone finds out. Pornography, however, is different. It can remain a secret sexual sin for decades—even a lifetime.

What is pornography? And why is it such a secret sin?

Pornography is defined as 'sexually-explicit media that are intended primarily to sexually arouse the audience'.[73]

160

73   Malamuth, N 2001, 'Pornography' in Smelser, NJ & Baltes, PB (eds), *International Encyclopedia of Social and Behavioral Sciences*, Elsevier, Amsterdam, pp. 11816–11821.

'Sexually-explicit' representations include images of female or male nudity or semi-nudity, implied sexual activity and actual sexual activity. So internet images and videos, erotic literature and sexually-explicit television shows and games are all pornography. Amateur videos of real couples involved in a range of sexual activities are now freely available on YouTube. These too are pornography.

Pornography use was once considered a male concern. However we are seeing increasing numbers of women hooked on pornographic literature and television shows masquerading as erotica. One of the current multimillion-dollar-earning erotic fiction stories portrays a female virgin and an older male sadomasochistic and obsessive control freak. This too is pornography.

There are two ways in which pornography slips under the radar of sexual sin. Firstly, pornography users find excuses and motivations for their behaviour. These are lies implanted in our consciousness by Satan. Here's some of what we hear as therapists:

- *Minimalisation:* 'I look, but only very occasionally'; 'I don't search for the hard stuff'; 'I'm not doing anything wrong; it's not like I'm being unfaithful to my wife'; 'It's no big deal is it?'
- *Normalisation:* 'Everybody does it'; 'It's just a boy thing'; 'It's mainstream stuff these days'.
- *Rationalisation:* 'I am so stressed at work; I deserve some pleasure'; 'My wife won't give me sex. What am I supposed to do?'; 'It's about female empowerment isn't it? Boys watch pornography. Why shouldn't we read erotic stories?'
- *Celebration:* 'It will help our lovemaking'; 'I learned all about sex from pornography'; 'Isn't it what all women want?'

And secondly, by its sheer ubiquitous nature, pornography panders to and encourages secrecy. Therapists call this the 'triple A engine': Accessibility, Affordability and Anonymity.

- *Accessibility:* the internet brings pornography right into the private corners of your home or office at high speeds, or right into your palm via your phone.
- *Affordability:* pornography is relatively cheap or free online.
- *Anonymity:* no-one has to know that you use it; it is your secret private activity.

It takes self-control, integrity and godliness for a person, man or woman, to be countercultural enough to turn away from the temptation.

Pornography use removes sex from its God-given setting and depicts it in the opposite way—as a temporary, depersonalised experience of instant, selfish self-gratification—stripped of any trace of relationship. It doesn't teach men to serve, honour and cherish their wives in a way that fosters romance. Pornography trains men to be consumers, to treat sex as a commodity. By masturbating to pornography, the user is wiring the brain to get a quick sexual high of orgasm and to bond with the image and activity.

A man who has learned his scripts from pornography struggles to adapt to a less than 'perfect' female body with normal genitalia. He may ask his wife to change her body in ways that fit his pornographic aesthetic, going from requests for a complete pubic hair removal to plastic surgery on her breasts and vulva. Or else he may request that she engage in sexual activities and behaviours that pornography has wired into his brain. The wife of a man whose sexual desire is pornified struggles with a deep feeling of rejection and loss of self-worth. There is also anger and feelings of being used and abused that come from being asked to do things that she feels are unnatural and reflect what porn stars do. This is not a healthy platform for marriage. Similarly, a wife whose sexual expectations are moulded by erotic literature of extreme sexual acts may find regular sexual activity with her husband stifling and boring.

You would realise by now that pornography use has no place in a Christian marriage. If you or your spouse is into pornography, please ask for help from your church or a therapist. I have given you some guidelines in Appendix 4. Tolerance of pornography use by one or both partners will lead to an increase in use of more explicit and variant pornography. Ultimately, 'just looking' may not be enough. Many porn users end up with sex workers, or in adulterous liaisons.

4. Dealing with infidelity

Firstly, what is infidelity? Is admiring an attractive woman you pass on the street considered to be adultery? What about the woman who enjoys watching the mud-covered, testosterone-filled bodies at a rugby match? Or even that special friendship two marrieds have at work?

Infidelity is defined as 'sexual intimacy with anyone who isn't your spouse'. This intimacy need not be intercourse; it could be any form of bodily contact that is associated with, or is likely to escalate to, deeper levels. In this age of electronic messaging, it could also be an exchange of sexual communications (email or phone texts) or photographs.

Virtual sex via cyber chat rooms and telephone are infidelity to your spouse. Whereas non-sexual intimate friendships with the opposite sex are possible and are in fact healthy, great care needs to be taken when the conversations begin to drift towards sexual intimacies and flirtation. This is especially so if the relationship is one that the spouse does not know about.

The surge of testosterone-fuelled desire or even feelings of dopamine-induced romantic attraction are not in themselves sinful. These are a biological reaction to something the brain finds appealing. And the human body, created in the image of God, is an attractive object. The initial feeling is not the sin—it is *dwelling* on it, developing it into a fantasy and even a masturbatory stimulus that turns it into lust. It is taking the 'she is beautiful' thought and converting it into 'I would like to have sex with her' that Jesus condemned (Matthew 5:27–29). Jesus even suggested that it is better to be without a part of your body than to lust after someone who is not your spouse!

When it comes to other sex friendships, boundaries are important and wisdom is called for in deciding the point at which a chat over morning coffee turns into flirtation and then seduction. Sex is a powerful arrow in Satan's quiver—be careful how you deal with it. Get your armour on. A great biblical example of this is Joseph's response to the invitation of Potiphar's wife (Genesis 39). He refused to give in to the temptation. We read that 'though she spoke to Joseph day after day, he refused to go to bed with her or even be with her' (Genesis 39:10).

The most alluring of distorted desires is that which draws a person away from the one they are committed to. One person in the relationship feels drawn to someone else. Is this love? Or is it lust? Is it that this new person, rather than your spouse, is your true soul mate? Should you leave your marriage for this person? Or just have a discreet affair?

Whatever way we look at it—whatever the reason we give, whether it is flirtation or physical intimacy—infidelity is a sexual sin. This, however, is not the message we hear from the world around us. Billboards proclaim: 'Life is short. Have an affair'. Websites created exclusively for adulterous liaisons[74] proclaim that 'every 20 seconds someone joins looking for a discreet affair'. Popular magazines and books celebrate the excitement of infidelity. They give you excuses: 'you were bored; your needs were not met by your spouse; and your new lover really understands you', or 'what harm can it do if your spouse doesn't know about it?' And yet, any couples counsellor will tell you of the pain and remorse that adultery causes, and the failed marriages that ensue.

The Bible tells us that adultery is loathsome to God (Jeremiah 3; Ezekiel 16; Matthew 5:27–29; Matthew 15:19). 'You shall not commit adultery', God says (Exodus 20:14). These are not the words of a conservative prig. Rather, they are the words of a generous God whose commandments are not burdensome, but wise and good. God created sex to be fun, wholesome and satisfying in a male–female covenant commitment of marriage. It is meant to be a Song of Songs experience of one-flesh fun. Outside of this, it is harmful to the relationship and painful to the individual.

Why and how are we drawn to someone other than our spouse?

74   Gannon, G 2012, 'Natural born cheaters?', *The Sydney Morning Herald*, viewed May 6 2013, <http://www.smh.com.au/lifestyle/life/natural-born-cheaters-20120807-23rmn.html>.

The characteristics that make a person attractive to us are influenced by our innate nature and life experience. Therefore the person who was the ultimate in sexiness to us when we were 18 may seem ho-hum when we are 28 or 48 or even 68. Sometimes the 'other' may be similar in many ways to the person we are married to. And sometimes even less good-looking or charming.

What's happening here? This is where we go back to brain chemistry. Sex scientists tell us that there are different systems in the brain for sexual desire, falling in love and attachment. This means that we could be deeply bonded and attached to one person, and be sexually turned on by, or even fall in love with, another. And sometimes for reasons we cannot consciously fathom.

So, if this is what the brain is set up to do, why don't more of us cheat on our marriage partners? It's the brain again, specifically the decision-making frontal and parietal lobes of our cerebral cortex. It enables us to make a decision as to what we do with the sexual pull to someone other than our spouse.

Cheating is a choice.

Although all animals have what is called a forebrain, we humans have the largest and most complex. It is the seat of the executive function of decision-making. It is where we process the feelings of emotion, sexual attraction and love, and filter these through our values and moral and religious beliefs. It is, in a way, the control point for monogamous behaviour.

To be found sexually attractive by, and be sexually attracted to, someone other than your spouse is an ego boost and an exciting prospect. However, faithfulness and fidelity is a choice. Thank God for the inhibitory functions of the cerebral cortex!

Is it any wonder that the writer of Proverbs spent a whole chapter on the seductive charms of the adulterous woman and how to resist her? (Proverbs 7)

The Apostle Paul was aware of the active nature of rejecting the seductive charm of affairs. 'Flee', he wrote to the Corinthians—don't bond your body with anyone other than your wife (1 Corinthians 6:15–20).

But, what happens to a marriage rocked by infidelity? Can a hurt spouse forgive? Forgiving an adulterous husband or wife is difficult and painful. It needs an assurance of God's grace in the lives of both partners. Paul also wrote, 'Forgive as the Lord forgave you' (Colossians 3:13).

It is hard work to let go of the feelings of rejection and anger brought about by infidelity. You cannot do it by yourself. It will take time to re-establish trust in your relationship. You need the counsel of wiser, older Christian couples. Couples therapy with a professional counsellor is always an option. Just remember that God can and will forgive every sin and every repentant sinner. By committing adultery, your spouse has sinned against you but ultimately, as King David recognised, all sin is against God (Psalm 51:3–4).

5. Sex after babies

In Genesis we learn that God made man in his image. He made them male and female, wonderfully and excitingly complementary in structure and function. And he gave them the joyous gift of sex with the command that they use it for procreation, and have fun doing it.

In a Christian marriage, children are a blessing and not an inconvenience or a burden. The writers of the Psalms said, 'your wife will be like a fruitful vine within your house; your children will be like olive shoots round your table' (128:3), and 'then our sons in their youth will be like well-nurtured plants, and our daughters will be like pillars carved to adorn a palace' (Psalm 144:12). Yes, we love our children. As Christian parents we work hard to nurture them in God's way.

How do we deal with the little blessings when they get in the way of our sex life?

In our scenarios, Jenny with her 'three little monsters' and Indrani with her mother-in-law caring for her daughters give us a taste of the problem.

Parenting is wonderful. But it is a tiring and time-consuming job to put little children to bed. Some parents even let them into their bed to make it easier. Can you think of a more effective libido-killer?

Having sex while children are in the house is definitely not the same as having sex without children nearby. When you're alone in the house, anything goes. You can have sex in your bed, on the floor, on the couch, on the kitchen bench, in the pool, even hanging from the chandeliers. When you have children or, like Indrani, extended family living with you, you need to plan ahead.

It is fine and healthy for children to see you, their parents, being sexually intimate, cuddling and kissing. It lays a strong foundation for family intimacy. Include them in cuddles occasionally. Children who feel that there is love in the family grow up secure and unafraid to show love to others. So go ahead—hug your spouse at the kitchen sink.

However, it is unnecessary and sometimes traumatic for children (particularly young children) to see their parents having full-on sexual intercourse.

So, what should you do? Here's some practical advice.

♥ Keep the relational boundaries of husband and wife separate from those of mother and father.

When did you stop calling your husband by name and start addressing him as 'Daddy'? When did that sexy girl you married stop being your 'angel' and turn into 'Mum'? Parenting is wonderful, but it is not sexy.

♥ Make time for each other.

This may seem obvious, but when there are children it takes some organisation. Find a babysitter. Form a group of parents with small kids and schedule 'date nights' for each of the parents.

♥ Keep the flame alive.

Sometimes one or both of you may be too tired for a full-blown active night of lovemaking. Learn to vary your sexual intimacy. Sometimes a quickie sexual intercourse can be calming (thanks to all the endorphins and oxytocin). At other times it may be a shower together, a body massage, or mutual touching may be just the answer. Talk. Change what you do and where. Determine what is best for both of you. Be patient.

♥ Get a lock for the door.

Children are never too young to understand the difference between public and private. Even toddlers can learn to knock on a shut door. Older kids may deduce the meaning of the locked bedroom door, but that won't harm them one bit!

So go ahead, being a good lover to your spouse will make you both better able to cope with the pressures of parenting.

6. When procreation becomes a chore rather than a pleasure

In a time when the age of people getting married is rising and women are postponing having children into their 30s and sometimes their 40s, it would be remiss of us not to mention the effect of infertility on sexual intimacy.

In the scenario at the beginning of Chapter 7, Indrani hints at the pressure to have a baby, and, in her case, a son. She speaks of the calendar watching for the fertile days of her menstrual cycle as a libido-killer.

According to recent US statistics, 6% of married women aged 15–44 are infertile.[75] One in six Australian couples is said to suffer infertility[76]—that is, unable to get pregnant after one year of trying.

How does the pressure and stress of waiting for the woman's fertile period, and the repeated disappointment of menstruation as a sign of another 'failure', affect marital intimacy and sex? What about the treatment methods of induced ovulation, hormone treatment and sometimes surgery and in-vitro fertilisation?

75   CDC FastStats, viewed June 10 2013, <http://www.cdc.gov/nchs/fastats/fertile.htm>.
76   Unreferenced data from the Fertility Society of Australia website, June 10 2011, <http://www.fertilitysociety.com.au/>.

Researchers tell us that the diagnosis of infertility and its management cause a range of sexual difficulties in couples, mainly in the female partner.[77] Sexual desire is the first to decrease. In some men, the pressure to get an erection on schedule may result in erectile dysfunction.

How should a Christian couple deal with this? This is a very large topic and we cannot explore it in depth here, but there are three broad principles to consider:

1. God is in charge, and will work out everything for your best and to his glory (Romans 8:28).
2. Your marriage is about more than procreation; it is an image of Christ and his Church to the world. How you deal with the emotional pain—the highs and troughs of this experience—will showcase the Christlikeness of your marriage to the world.
3. Sexual intimacy between married couples is for procreation and for mutual bonding. Remember this second purpose as you strive to accomplish the first.

So, keep the fires of intimacy burning between you. Fan it on the days when you feel the lowest. Use all the skills we have discussed. Talk about your feelings. Be sensual and in the moment together. Keep your relationship close and Christlike. And know that the God who brought you together as man and wife has a purpose for your marriage.

---

77   Wischmann, TH 2010, 'Original research—Couples sexual dysfunction: Sexual disorders in Infertile couples', *Journal of Sexual Medicine,* 7, pp. 1868–1876.

7. Many other questions

There are many other issues about sex and sensuality in marriage that we haven't discussed. Here are a couple.

♥ Sexual intimacy during pregnancy

In a normal pregnancy, sexual intimacy and intercourse can be continued as long as the couple desire and the woman feels comfortable. However, it is best to discuss this with your doctor or obstetrician.

♥ Problems of sexual function

We discussed discrepant sexual desire, and vaginismus in the female. Sometimes the male partner develops problems of erection (erectile dysfunction) or ejaculation (premature ejaculation, retarded ejaculation). Sometimes the causes of these are psychological. We discuss some of these in the next section. However, if you have any of these concerns in your marriage, we would urge you to consult with your doctor immediately. Sexual problems, especially erectile dysfunction, can be the first sign of an underlying illness such as heart disease or diabetes mellitus.

Take-away messages

- Sex in marriage honours the spouse and mirrors the relationship of Christ and the Church.
- Good sex and healthy sexual intimacy in marriage begins with honest communication about expectations and perceptions between the couple.
- Sexual activities in marriage can be varied and wonderful. They must, however, be other-honouring and edifying, rather than motivated by a selfish need for gratification.
- Common sexual concerns of desire discrepancy and a search for more passion in marriage can usually be solved with knowledge of the sexual response and the practise of other-focused loving.
- More difficult sexual concerns of pornography use and infidelity need help from the Church family or trained professionals.
- Marriage is a process of couple growth and sanctification. Grace and forgiveness form a foundation for lifelong trust.

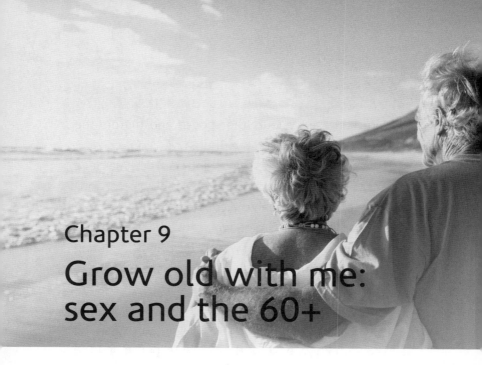

Chapter 9
Grow old with me: sex and the 60+

This is a section that everyone should read. If you belong to the 60+ club—welcome! This chapter is just for you. If you are just engaged to be married, newlywed or married with little children, 60+ years will seem a long way into the future. But this chapter is important to you too. Firstly, you are surrounded by older adults. Look around you—there are parents and grandparents, aunties and uncles, and the older people in your church. Knowingly and unknowingly, they are your role models for behaviour, sexual intimacy and other relationships. Secondly, you too are ageing and, like it or not, someday you will be in the 60+ club! Walk in the shoes of a golden oldie for a while and read on.

> *Rejoice in the wife of your youth. A loving doe, a graceful deer—may her breasts satisfy you always, may you ever be intoxicated with her love.* (Proverbs 5:18–19)

Can you continue the intoxication of love in marriage into your 60s, 70s and even 90s to a time when neither of you are as nimble as a deer nor supple as a doe? What happens when, as the writer of Ecclesiastes describes, *the years approach when you will say, 'I find no pleasure in them'* (12:1)? The time *when the almond tree blossoms and the grasshopper drags itself along and desire no longer is stirred* (12:5)?

Does sex change with age? Does it cease? Or could it get better? Is sexual behaviour an arena in which older Christian couples are challenged to nurture the young? As the psalmist says:

> *Since my youth, God, you have taught me, and to this day I declare your marvellous deeds. Even when I am old and grey, do not forsake me, my God, till I declare your power to the next generation, your mighty acts to all who are to come.* (71:17–18)

This is what we will explore in this chapter.

Are older people sexually active?

Researchers tell us that men and women remain sexually active into their 70s and 80s. Ageing-related physical changes do not necessarily lead to a decline in sexual function. Good physical and mental health, positive attitudes toward sex in later life, and access to a healthy partner are all associated with continued sexual activity.[78]

78 DeLamater, J 2012, 'Sexual expression in later life: A review and synthesis', *Journal of Sex Research*, 49, 2–3, pp. 125–141.

Younger people however continue to see the elderly as asexual. Teenagers find the thought of sexy grandparents 'gross' and many don't believe their parents have sex. Even health professionals neglect to inquire about sexual practices in their elderly clients.[79]

The 60+ of today were the baby boomers of yesteryear, and they are loath to lose their sexual identity. Sexual change associated with 'normal' ageing is no longer accepted as what determines behaviour. Today we can 're-sex' ageing bodies to align them with the culturally dominant notion of ageless sexual prowess. It is no longer the grey-haired senior driving the red Lamborghini in an attempt to regain his lost youth. Rather it is men and women remaining in a state of pseudo-youth in both body and function.

The sexy seniors of the 21st century have grasped the challenge to remain sexually active. A US study[80] reported that 84% of men aged 57–64 had participated in sexual activity in the previous 12 months, compared with 67% among 65–74-year-olds and 39% among 75–84-year-olds. Among women, 62% of those aged 57–64, 40% aged 65–74 and 17% of 75–84-year-olds had also reported sexual activity in that 12-month period. True, we have less sex, but we're still doing well into our 80s and beyond!

Researchers also tell us that high rates of divorce and partner change in the older age groups have resulted in

79 Snyder, RJ & Zweig, RA 2010, 'Medical and psychology students' knowledge and attitudes regarding aging and sexuality', Gerontology & Geriatrics Education, 31:3, pp.235–255.
80 Lindau, ST, Schumm, LP, Laumann, EO, Levinson, W, O'Muircheartaigh C & Waite, LJ 2007, 'A study of sexuality and health among older adults in the United States', New England Journal of Medicine, 357, pp. 762–774.

an increase of sexually transmitted infections.[81] Rates of chlamydia, gonorrhoea and syphilis have doubled for people in their 50s, 60s and 70s in the past decade.[82] These are the baby boomers who equated safe sex with avoiding pregnancy, rather than preventing STIs. They see no need for protection when having postmenopausal fun.

Medical science has responded to the perceived demand of these 'sexy seniors'. Hormonal treatment of menopause and male andropause delays ageing. The development of biomedical interventions for sexual dysfunctions (such as erectile dysfunction and low libido) has kept older people sexually active and virile. Plastic surgery gives you the means to look as good, perhaps even better, than you did when you were young. And drugs, implants and pumps enable you to have sex—penetrative sex—into old age. The launch of the first medications for erectile dysfunction was heralded with announcements like, 'Now you can have sex, when, where and how you want it, dependably and reliably, even if you're 100 and your partner's 102'.[83] Today, drug firms scramble for a 'pink Viagra' that would act as a desire booster for women at any age. The media are ever ready to report on the purported benefits of regular sex in reducing the risk of heart attack, boosting the immune system, lowering the risk of prostate cancer, and preventing everything from wrinkles

81   Minichiello, V, Hawkes, G & Pitts, M 2011, 'HIV, sexually transmitted infections, and sexuality in later life', Current Infectious Disease Reports, 13, 2, pp. 182–187.
82   Gann, C 2012, 'Sex life of older adults and rising STDs', ABC News Online, viewed May 20 2013, <http://abcnews.go.com/blogs/health/2012/02/03/older-people-getting-busy-and-getting-stds/>.
83   Vaughn, SC, 1998, Viagra: A Guide To The Phenomenal Potency Promoting Drug, Pocket Books, New York, p. 14.

to incontinence.[84] Researchers tell us that 'regular consensual sexual expression' contributes to physical and psychological wellbeing, and may reduce physical and mental health problems associated with ageing, correlated with a higher quality of intimate relationships, lower rates of depressive symptoms, improved cardiovascular health, even a loss of weight.[85]

We are staying sexually active into our old age. But must we? Should we?

How should Christians approach sexuality and sexual function as we age?

A biblical basis for sexual intimacy and ageing

Does the Bible give us any guidelines on sexuality in older men and women?

The patriarchs of the Old Testament were sexually active to a mature age. After all, Abraham was 100 years old and Sarah, 90 when she gave birth to Isaac (Genesis 17:17). Jacob, we read, loved Joseph because he was born to him in his old age (Genesis 37:3). In the New Testament, John the Baptist was born to Zechariah and Elizabeth when they were very old (Luke 1:7).

But these were God's chosen people, fertile beyond what we would consider menopause. What about a married couple today who are past procreative age? Does the Bible give us any guidelines?

84   See, for example, Health Canada's fact sheet on 'Seniors and Aging–Sexual Activity', which reiterates the suggestions of more sex equalling less pain, stronger bones, better immune systems, and fewer wrinkles. <http://www.hc-sc.gc.ca/hl-vs/iyh-vsv/life-vie/seniors-aines-eng.php#th>. Viewed May 20 2013.
85   DeLamater, J, ibid.

Let's go back to Genesis 1 and 2. We are created in the image of God, as embodied beings, male and female, made for relationship with the other. We long for this. We hunger for it and would starve without it. This does not change with age. Rather, it is the purpose and end point of intimate relationships that change with age. Once the procreative potential is past, sexual intimacy becomes solely an activity of a one-flesh, naked and no-shame bonding between husband and wife. The hunger for that continues.

With the end point of pregnancy totally removed, sexual activity can focus on intimacy rather than intercourse. There may be a choice of any activity, or this choice may be governed by physical changes, illness or other disability.

As older Christian couples, whether as parents, grandparents, aunties or uncles, you are in a position to model and teach the younger generation(s) the meaning of true sexual intimacy and commitment in marriage. An intimacy based on commitment and love, not erotic, orgasmic self-gratification.

In his letter, Paul instructed Titus to advise the older members of his church as follows:

> *Teach the older women to be reverent in the way they live, not to be slanderers or addicted to much wine, but to teach what is good. Then they can urge the younger women to love their husbands and children, to be self-controlled and pure, to be busy at home, to be kind, and to be subject to their husbands, so that no one will malign the word of God. Similarly, encourage the young men to be self-controlled. In everything set them an example by doing what is good. (Titus 2:3–7)*

And elsewhere (Deuteronomy 6:6–7; Proverbs 22:6) we are clearly instructed on the role of parents and grandparents in nurturing godly children.

You need to 'walk the walk and talk the talk' in your relationships and sexual intimacy. Young people are faced with the media's portrayal of the perfect body and perfect sex. Today's individualistic society tells them to place themselves first and do whatever it takes to fulfil their desires for sex or whatever. 'Your needs must be met immediately', they are told. It is more important now than ever for older caring Christian couples to nurture our youth. The living out of faithfulness and loving intimacy by older Christian couples will be a far better form of sex education than anything our children or grandchildren will receive from school, their peers or the media.

Is your relationship a model to the next generation?

The practicality of living and loving in old age

You may believe that having grown up in the age of sex, drugs and rock and roll, you know it all. In actual fact, many people of your generation are woefully ignorant of the reality of ageing sexually and are unprepared to deal with it.

Christian couples are especially vulnerable. You have tried your best to keep your thoughts and minds pure (Philippians 4:8). As a couple you have avoided pornography and erotic literature, impure fantasies and language (Colossians 3:7–8). You have attempted to live the life that the Apostle Paul called you to live as husband and wife in Ephesians 5. Now you need help to understand and interpret the changes and challenges of ageing.

Firstly, we need to be clear that intimacy and sexuality are basic human needs that are intrinsic to people's sense of self and wellbeing. Regardless of age, individuals require companionship, intimacy and love. Sexuality and ageing are *not* incompatible.

There are two groups of sexy seniors.

The first is those between the ages of 60 and about 75. You are the newly retired. The children have left home. You are relatively fit, and have freedom and the money to live your life anyway you wish.

True, it is an age of biological decline: a time of wrinkles, grey hair, arthritis pains, menopause, and decreased libido. You may pay more attention to advertisements about Cialis and Viagra than Coke ads! And you may be taking medicines for diabetes, high cholesterol and hypertension.

And then there are the couples in their late 70s, 80s and 90s. It's a time of decreased mobility, canes, hernia surgery and cataracts. Functions are now slowing down, and this includes sexual function. And even with what function is left, a sexual partner may not be available. Assisted care becomes a reality and a move to a nursing home with the sterile, impersonal environment, and asexuality of incontinence and pads looms ahead. For many in this age the basic human right of intimacy is often denied, ignored or stigmatised. For older people with dementia the problem is even worse: they face the 'double jeopardy' of being old and cognitively impaired.

The challenges are broadly the same in both groups: the bodily changes of ageing in a changing relational and family context, and the need to reframe expectations. The specifics differ. So, we will discuss each age group separately.

Sex and the baby boomer generations (60–75 years)

Ageing and the sexual body

Male and female genitalia change with age. In men, erections take longer to achieve and, when they do occur, could be smaller and not as rigid. There is also a decrease in sensation on the penile skin. Men report fewer sleep erections and less forceful ejaculations. The frequency of occasional erectile problems and even complete erectile dysfunction increases with age.

In a large cross-national study[86] with men over 40 years of age, around 30% of men reported erectile dysfunction (ED) and 6% severe orgasmic impairment, both of which were closely associated with increasing age and illnesses such as hypertension, obesity and heart disease. Interestingly, only 38% of men with ED said they were concerned about it. Further, in those over 70 years of age, about 60% of those with ED said they had enjoyed other forms of sexual activity such as petting and mutual masturbation, confirming that there are other ways to get sexual gratification that do not require a good erection, and sex is more than just penis-in-vagina intercourse.

It is important to note that the decrease or loss of erection at any age could be a barometer for the onset of cardiovascular disease, hypertension, diabetes, prostate hypertrophy and

---

86   Corona, G, Lee, DM, Forti, G, O'Connor, DB, Maggi, M, O'Neill, TW, Pendleton, N, Bartfai, G, Boonen, S, Casanueva, FF, Finn, JD, Giwercman, A, Han, TS, Huhtaniemi, IT, Kula, K, Lean, MEJ, Punab, M, Silman, AJ, Vanderschueren, D, Wu, FCW & the EMAS Study Group 2010, 'Age-related changes in general and sexual health in middle-aged and older men: Results from the European Male Ageing Study (EMAS)', *Journal of Sexual Medicine*, 7, pp. 1362–1380.

other illnesses. Some general practitioners routinely ask about sexual function, others don't. If you think you have a sexual problem, bring it up with your doctor. Don't be embarrassed. It may save your life.

As you age, you are likely to be taking some form of medication. Drugs for anxiety (benzodiazepines), depression (selective serotonin reuptake inhibitors), and a range of other antipsychotics affect sexual desire and arousal in men and women. Some drugs used in heart disease such as beta-blockers and some diuretics are also thought to have effects on sexual function. Surgical procedures like radical prostatectomy also affect sexual function in men.

For a woman, menopause is a complex period of transition associated with hormonal, physical, psychological as well as social adjustments. Women experience vaginal dryness and atrophy due to the gradual decline in levels of oestrogen in the body. The tissues of the vulva get less engorged during sex. It is estimated that as many as 60% of postmenopausal women experience these conditions.[87] The consequences, however, vary a great deal. Serious symptoms include aches and itching in the vulva and vagina, burning, and pain during penetrative sex (dyspareunia). Orgasms become less frequent and less intense. Some women take longer to be sexually aroused. Interestingly, some postmenopausal women, released from the pressure of pregnancy, report feeling more sexual desire.

What does this tell us about sex and ageing? It tells us that our bodies will only last a finite time on earth. They slow down

87   DeLamater, J, ibid.

and change with age. However, we know that even though old age causes our bodies to fail, God is there to uphold us (Isaiah 46:4). He who made us will carry and sustain us to the end.

What does this mean for your sex life as a couple? How should you deal with the slowing of your sexual functions while you are still reasonably fit and able to enjoy them?

Dealing with change

In terms of sexuality and function, you can respond to the outworking of this slowing down in one of two ways:

1. You can spend time and money on medication and surgery to attain a semblance of your youthful sexual function with the accompanying penetrative sex.
2. You can reframe your thinking to accept a new norm of sexuality.

Let's look first at the options available to manage and improve sexual function. There are a range of medical and surgical modalities available for male sexual dysfunctions. They range from the much publicised drugs of a class called PDE5 inhibitors (Cialis, Levitra, Viagra) for erectile dysfunction (sometimes called impotence) and drugs for the treatment of premature ejaculation (currently selective serotonin reuptake inhibitors [SSRIs] and tricyclic antidepressants); through to vacuum pumps, injections into the penis and the surgical insertion of prostheses. There is much less for women, although there is an ongoing search for a pink Viagra. The management of female sexual concerns is largely by behaviour modification methods.

Should Christian couples use sexual medications to re-establish penetrative sexual function lost in ageing, illness and surgery?

There is nothing inherently sinful in turning to medication to improve your sex life. Your doctor or a sex therapist could advise you on the options available. However, I would recommend that couples work by two principles.

Firstly, whose decision is it? In a marriage relationship your body is not your own. In 1 Corinthians 7:4, Paul says, *the wife does not have authority over her own body but yields it to her husband. In the same way, the husband does not have authority over his own body but yields it to his wife.* It is therefore important that any decision is a joint decision between the couple. If you both want it, can afford it and it is medically approved by your doctor—go for it.

This verse is preceded by *the husband should fulfil his marital duty to his wife, and likewise the wife to her husband* (1 Corinthians 7:3). So, does this fulfilment of marital duties and the sexual satisfaction that follows suggest a need for penetrative sexual intercourse? The research indicates not.[88] Older couples report obtaining sexual pleasure and satisfaction from activities that are not conventionally sexual. As we get older, holding, touching, cuddling, and generally being intimate and close without having sex take on a deeper significance, with even activities such as gardening and 'playing footsy under the table' taking on an aura of sensuality. So discuss your options for activities as a couple carefully before making the decision.

Secondly, why are you doing it? What is your motivation?

---

88   Hinchliff, S, & Gott, M 2004, 'Intimacy, commitment and adaptation: Sexual relationships within long-term marriages', *Journal of Social & Personal Relationships*, 21, pp. 595–609.

In 1 Corinthians 6:12 Paul says, *'I have the right to do anything', you say—but not everything is beneficial. 'I have the right to do anything'—but I will not be mastered by anything.*

The question then should not be, 'Am I permitted to do this as a Christian?' but rather, 'am I (or are we as a couple) a slave to this act? Is our sexual activity becoming our master instead of a blessing? Is it an idol? Is this activity building us up as a couple to serve God better?' Maybe even, 'could the money we are using for this procedure be used instead for building up God's kingdom?'

And again in 1 Corinthians 10:23, *'I have the right to do anything', you say—but not everything is beneficial. 'I have the right to do anything'—but not everything is constructive.*

Constructive things are those that build others up in their faith. Is what you plan to do in your couple sex life witness to God's glory in your life? How does this model your life and relationship to your children, grandchildren and the Church? Is the expense and energy spent on penile implants, breast enhancement and Botox the example you want to set of godly choices to family and other young people in the church community?

The second option would be to reframe your sexuality and sexual intimacy behaviour.

Reframed attitudes to sexual intimacy

Ageing doesn't end sexuality; it just changes it. It changes both the context and the intention of sexual activity and intimacy. We need to understand this. And to explore what this changing spectrum of intimacy means to individual and couple sexuality, and to the marriage relationship. We need to look critically at the secular rhetoric of 'ageless sexual bodies' and sexuality as 'intercourse on demand' and consider God's countercultural context, in which intimacy rather than intercourse continues 'till death do us part' as a symbol of our covenantal commitment to each other.

To do this, we need to move from intimacy equals intercourse to a model of intimacy that encompasses the whole array of sensualities, like those practised by the married couple in the Song of Songs: *The mandrakes send out their fragrance, and at our door is every delicacy, both new and old, that I have stored up for you, my beloved.* (7:13)

There are stored-up treasures of sensuality that a couple may have never taken time to savour. With the children gone and time to spare, now is the time when a couple could explore every stored-up delicacy. Relive loving things you did early in life. Be adventurous. It will bring back the dopamine and norepinephrine surge. Testosterone may be low but you'll have that loving feeling of sexual desire again.

And toss out the range of common myths on sex and ageing.

❤ Older people are asexual: WRONG

If you are 60+, you know that this is not true. This is supported by the data we have discussed above. Sexual satisfaction for older couples depends more on the overall quality of the relationship than it does for younger couples. Sexual desire keeps going. Your libido may be decreased, but it's still there. Rediscover it. Fan the embers.

Older men take longer to feel turned on. The transition to slower arousal can be disconcerting, but it means that the sexual discord of youth can evolve into new sexual harmony. The sexual response cycles now move together. Compared to when you were young lovers, you may find that you are more sexually in sync. Enjoy it.

If you want to continue penetrative sex, you will have to adapt. So her vagina is dry, use a lubricant. Or try saliva as a lubricant. If his erection is floppy, change to a woman on top position and help the penis into the vagina. Or else, just forget intercourse and enjoy the sensuality of full body sexual intimacy.

Sexual intercourse is the end point of all sexual intimacy: WRONG

We have already discussed the range of activities that older couples engage in. Any and all of these activities could be a legitimate end point for sexual intimacy. Many older couples have a great sex life without having sexual intercourse. Discuss your preferences. The sensual discovery activities in Appendix 2 are a useful guide for exploring a range of sensuality stimuli.

Sex has to be spontaneous: WRONG

Our culture portrays sex as most gratifying when it is spontaneous. Television shows portray sex as a sort of mutual, instant, spontaneous combustion of sexual energy. However, portraying sex in this way leads to unrealistic expectations. If perfect and spontaneous sexual performances are expected by older couples, they will be disappointed and the performance anxiety will decrease the pleasure they get from sex.

Older couples need to plan sex most times. Sometimes it is a disability (arthritis) or illness that needs painkillers, or even some appliance like a stoma bag that needs to be cleaned. Other times it is just finding a time when you are both relaxed and not tired. You may have been used to sex last thing before bed. Now you are too tired. Why not have sex first thing in the morning?

♡ I am too ill or disabled to be sexual: WRONG

There is no illness or disability that makes a person totally asexual. Here are some common disabilities, and how they can be worked around sexually.

- *Arthritis:* Joint pain due to arthritis can make movement uncomfortable. Joint replacement surgery and drugs may relieve this pain. Exercise, rest, warm baths, and changing the position or even the timing of sexual activity can be helpful. To add to this, lovemaking is a great exercise to mobilise stiff joints.
- *Chronic pain:* Any constant pain can interfere with intimacy. Chronic pain does not have to be part of growing older and can be treated. But some pain medicines can interfere with sexual function. Talk with your doctor if you have unwanted side effects from any medication.
- *Chronic illness* like diabetes, heart disease and urinary problems. Whereas these may cause sexual dysfunctions, they do not mean an end to sexual intimacy. It is important for the couple to make a joint decision with the assistance of their doctor as to whether they wish to get medical intervention or work around the concern with non-penetrative sexual intimacy.
- *Incontinence:* Loss of bladder control or leaking of urine may occur with ageing. Passing urine before and immediately

after sexual activity will help. Also, changing the position so as not to put pressure on the bladder is helpful.

- *Stroke and other forms of paralysis:* A change in positions or medical devices may help people with ongoing weakness or paralysis to have sexual intimacy. Some people with paralysis from the waist down are still able to experience orgasm and pleasure.

In a strong Christian marriage that glorifies God, a couple's enjoyment of one another takes place on a long continuum of romantic affection and expression within the safe boundary of covenant commitment. Towards one end are things like companionship and fellowship. At the other end of the continuum are things like playful intimacy and really serious sex. Relationships in older couples move across this continuum like a concert pianist playing a keyboard. The result could be a wonderful symphony of sexual activity.

Take-away messages

- Consider your sexual intimacy and couple relationship both as an activity of bonding between you and an example to the young people around you.
- Redefine your relationship to include the array of sexually intimate activities.
- Don't let illness and disability turn you off sexual activity.
- Put away the myth of the sexless aged and live a full life of sexual intimacy with your spouse.

Sex and the 75+

Consider the words we use to describe this age group of ageing adults: the winter of life, decrepit, dotage, senile, geriatric, hoary, past one's prime, long in the tooth, one foot in the grave. I'm sure you can think of many more. What perceptions of ageing do these terms bring to mind? And how do you think it would affect the self-worth of an older person to carry these labels? Even the positive terms like doyen, ripe old age and venerable are couched in years of life and capability.

The psalmist tells us *the righteous will flourish like a palm tree, they will grow like a cedar of Lebanon; planted in the house of the Lord, they will flourish in the courts of our God. They will still bear fruit in old age, they will stay fresh and green, proclaiming, 'The Lord is upright; he is my Rock, and there is no wickedness in him'.* (92:12–15)

How do the aged bear fruit? How do you proclaim the goodness of God?

And for younger readers, how can you facilitate this in the older people in your personal and church family?

Here, we will consider these questions in the context of sexuality.

First, a word to those people aged 75+ reading this: each of you is unique. Your life situations vary. You may be still married and living with your partner in your own home, a retirement village or a nursing home. You may be married but separated from your life partner due to differential care needs. On the other hand, you may be single, having never had a partner, or having lost your spouse to death or divorce. Whoever you may be, the longing for sexual intimacy is normal. Again, each person's needs vary in terms of how much you desire intimacy.

For some it may be a fleeting thought of 'wouldn't it be nice if ...', and for others it may be an emptiness that haunts every waking moment.

Sex at any age is any mutually voluntary sexual activity with another person. It involves sexual contact, whether or not intercourse or orgasm occurs. When you were young, sex meant intercourse. But as you age, intimacy rather than intercourse becomes the norm. Researchers[89] tell us that as we get to the 75+ age, activities such as touching, hand-holding, embracing, hugging and kissing take precedence as satisfying acts of sexual intimacy over masturbation or intercourse. On the other hand, you may as a couple want to have, and be capable of having, sexual intercourse. That too is OK.

Don't feel guilty or ashamed that you desire this intimacy. If you are blessed with a spouse living with you, it is healthy and normal for your children and grandchildren to see you holding hands and kissing—whatever age you are.

What if you are single, never married, widowed or divorced? Or your spouse is alive and disabled? And you find yourself attracted to a person in the retirement village or nursing home? Here are a couple of questions to ask yourself before you get physically intimate.

1. Are you searching for friendship or sexual intimacy? Is it that you like spending time with the person? Enjoy their company? Or is it that being with them arouses you sexually?
2. Is the person you are attracted to as cognitively aware of

89   Elias, J & and Ryan, A 2011, 'A review and commentary on the factors that influence expressions of sexuality by older people in care homes', *Journal of Clinical Nursing*, 20, pp.1668–1676.

what is happening as you are? In other words, are you certain the other person does not have dementia or Alzheimer's?

3. Where do you want the relationship to lead?

If it is companionship you are looking for, then keep the intimacy light and avoid being alone together. Does this sound like the advice you gave your teenage children when they started dating? The same principles hold whatever age you may be. If your spouse is alive, any sexually intimate relationship with another person is infidelity. If you are single and think that you would like to continue the relationship to marriage then, just as you would tell your children to do, discuss it with another wise friend. Then go for it.

Finally, what about the solo sex of masturbation? Sometimes this may be the only outlet for sexual tension in a single person. Don't feel guilty or ashamed if you want this release. However, just as you advised your children, refrain from lustful thoughts and pornography as a stimulus.

♥ A word to younger readers

Now, a word of advice to our younger readers who have parents, grandparents, relatives and members of the church family in the 75+ age category: remember that the need for relationship and intimacy does not disappear in old age. If the situation arises that a person you know and care for is seeking sexual intimacy that you feel is inappropriate, ask yourself: why are you uncomfortable with this? Is it because you think the person is not cognitively able to make the decision? Or the relationship is in some way abusive? Or it is an act of infidelity? On the other hand is your discomfort the result of your personal biases and misconceptions of sexual intimacy and the elderly? Do you believe that your parent, grandparent or elderly friend has neither the ability nor even the right to desire sexual intimacy? Maybe it is a more selfish motive, such as the fear of losing your inheritance?

Examine your motives. Make yourself aware of the circumstances by discussing it with the person and their carer(s). You may find out that you are overreacting. What you see as sexual may be a need for friendship and companionship. It is the expression of the physical hunger every human feels for a caring touch rather than the clinical touch. Ask yourself: have you been there for this person? Have you taken the time and effort to provide them with friendship and companionship? Did you take time to hold their hand? Did you make an attempt to assuage the loneliness of old age by providing the intimacy of a hug? Look around your church community. Are you caring for the need for intimacy and companionship of the aged in the family? As we learn from Paul (1 Timothy 5:1-2), don't rebuke an older man harshly, but exhort him as if he were your father. And treat older women as you would your mothers. So, exhort if needed, but love with compassion always.

Walk in the shoes of your elderly relative or friend. You will be there someday. Jesus said we are to honour our parents and love God and our neighbour (Matthew 19:18–19). Ask yourself if your attitudes and actions are honouring and loving. Consult wise elders. Then act.

Take-away messages

- The need for relationships, close friendships and companionship remains until we die.
- It is normal to desire intimate touch—even sexual touch.
- Intimacy is not sinful if it isn't adulterous, abusive or lustful.
- Sexual intimacy and marriage is an option at any age.

Conclusion
The best sex for life

There are two strands of thought that have been held together in this book. In this conclusion, we invite you to reflect on your life as man and woman before God, and ask yourself where you stand as a married couple.

Firstly, the best sex comes from being outwardly focused toward your spouse. In the engagement period it is about honouring your fiancée or fiancé in thought and action. This builds a foundation of trustworthiness for the future. When you are newlyweds, it is other-focused loving that builds each other up in honesty and vulnerability, while encouraging the other to godliness, all the while enjoying God's gift of sex. When the children arrive and the pressures and anxieties of daily life threaten to swamp you, the best sex will be in that oasis of intimacy that you have carved out as a couple. Here you will build a safe place for you and your spouse to safeguard your marriage. This will help you model good relationships and sex to your children. And finally, when old age comes, the best sex will be built on your history of love and trust. It will be the beacon of intimacy that comforts and cheers you to the end.

Secondly, while marriage and sex are 'private' in that they belong exclusively to the couple, what happens between a husband and wife matters to the family, the small group Bible study, the Church and the community. And most importantly, it matters to God. For Christians, there is no private sexual sin. Therefore every thought and action in your sex life must be considered through the lens of God's pattern for sex that started in Genesis (Genesis 1–2) and will end in the new creation (Revelation 21). A relationship patterned on the covenant commitment of Jesus' love for his bride, the Church (Ephesians 5:22–33). Whether engaged to be married, married, or even in a post-marital state of being widowed or divorced, you need to be accountable for your sexual thoughts, decisions and actions to God and the people of God. Further, the Church is your spiritual family. As an engaged or married couple, you should be both humble enough to confess your sins and confident in the knowledge that you will have wise counsel there.

Don't feel discouraged if you feel that you are struggling in these areas. The Christian life is a path of growth in godliness. Sanctification in all aspects of our life, including our sex life, is a process. On earth, we may never be perfect. But as we practise Christlike virtues (Philippians 2:5–8) in our marriage, we will have the best sex for life.

Appendix 1:
Female external genitalia (Sexualia)

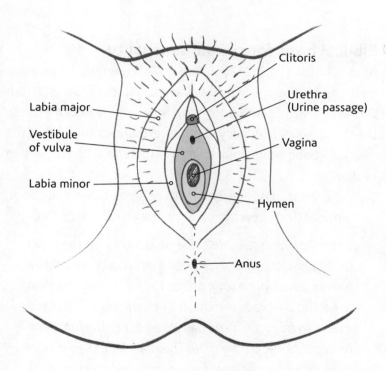

Appendix 2:
Sensual discovery pathway for couples

Biblical basis for couple sensuality

As a Christian couple you are in a committed covenant relationship. You recognise that sexual intimacy is a gift from God and a significant part of your marriage. You can express the joys of sexual intimacy without restraint, knowing that the marriage bond seals your love in a lifetime commitment to each other.

This is what these sensual discovery activities are all about. Consider God's description of marriage in Genesis 2:20–25:

> … for Adam no suitable helper was found. So the LORD God caused the man to fall into a deep sleep; and while he was sleeping, he took one of the man's ribs and then closed up the place with flesh. Then the Lord God made a woman from the rib he had taken out of the man, and he brought her to the man. The man said, 'This is now bone of my bones and flesh of my flesh; she shall be called "woman", for she was taken out of man'. That is why a man leaves his father and mother and is united to his wife, and they become one flesh. Adam and his wife were both naked, and they felt no shame.

God instituted marriage. And in marriage the naked and no-shame relationship of sexual intimacy is good. It is a physical, emotional and spiritual union in which Adam and Eve became one flesh.

We see Jesus quoting this in Matthew 19:4–6, and the Apostle Paul reinforcing it in Ephesians 5:31–32.

Timothy, speaking of false teachings, tells us that *everything God created is good*. It is an injunction to receive the good gift of sex with thanksgiving.

> *They (false teachers) forbid people to marry and order them to abstain from certain foods, which God created to be received with thanksgiving by those who believe and who know the truth. For everything God created is good, and nothing is to be rejected if it is received with thanksgiving, because it is consecrated by the word of God and prayer.* (1 Timothy 4:3–5)

Couples activity 1

Read the Genesis passage (Genesis 2:20–25) together, and reflect on the following *individually*:

1. What was Adam's response when God gave him his wife Eve? What does this tell you about how you as a couple could and should be able to respond to being sexually intimate?
2. What do you think it means to be in a naked and no-shame, one-flesh relationship as husband and wife?
3. What factors (family, friends, magazines, television ... anything) in your life have influenced how you feel about this? In what ways do your feelings about these issues

differ now from when you were single? Why do you think this is?

Make time to *share your thoughts* with each other.

Adam was excited when he saw Eve. She was just perfect for him. Although we don't hear of Eve's response, we can assume (from reading Song of Songs) that she too would have felt desire for him.

A 'naked and no-shame' relationship is one of total and unabashed trust. To be naked before another person is to be ultimately vulnerable. And to feel no shame in this act of shared intimacy is an act of trust—a blatant sharing of the body and emotions. Each act of sexual intimacy will be one where both husband and wife know that they will not be judged on the size and shape of their genitals or their performance in bed. Sex will be an act where mutual vulnerability will be celebrated and supported, and the wrinkles of ageing and associated changes in sexual function will be lovingly accepted. There will be no shame because covenant love covers a multitude of sins (1 Peter 4:8; 1 Corinthians 13:5).

In 1 Corinthians 7:4–6, Paul told the Church that the bodies of Eve and Adam belonged to each other. In other words, when it comes to sexual intimacy, it is good and right for the couple to engage in whole-body sharing. It is more, much more, than sexual intercourse. Sexual intercourse is a part of it. It is just not the obvious and constant end point.

Sometimes this couple sensuality is difficult for one or both partners. There are many reasons for this. The next activity gives you the space to discuss some of these.

Couples activity 2

Make time to discuss the following. Take time for each to share while the other listens. Then discuss the issues raised. Be honest. Keep calm. Take time out if you feel that either of you is getting upset.

Is there anything about (i) your body, (ii) how you feel about sex, or (iii) your relationship that forms a barrier to the 'naked and no-shame' relationship?

There are many experiences, from childhood and premarital sexual activity through to resentments in marriage, that set our sex scripts and rewire the sensuality circuits of the brain. One of the purposes of participating in this couple sensuality pathway activity is to gently change the wiring of these circuits. It is God's plan for you to be intimate as a couple—sexually and otherwise.

This activity of sharing may be painful for some couples. If it is, don't be ashamed to ask for help from an older Christian couple you trust. You can put the past behind you. The Apostle Paul spoke of the new person we become in Christ in his letters. Our sinful selves are part of the old. As man and woman before Christ, you can build new scripts of other-focused loving and new patterns of intimacy.

> You were taught, with regard to your former way of life, to put off your old self, which is being corrupted by its deceitful desires; to be made new in the attitude of your minds; and to put on the new self, created to be like God in true righteousness and holiness. (Ephesians 4:22–24)

Claim this regenerate newness in your couple sensuality and sex life. Understanding how your spouse feels about his or her body and sexual intimacy will enable you to be mindful of your own feelings and those of your spouse as you participate in the sexual discovery activities.[90]

Couples activity 3

The eight chapters of married loving in the Song of Songs are in the Bible for a purpose! They show how positive God is towards sex.

The lovers in the Song of Songs knew how to enjoy this sharing of the body. You can learn from this.

Read the first two chapters together (better still, read all eight). Note that sexual intercourse is not mentioned in it. Rather there is a profound enjoyment of each other's body in sight, smell, taste, touch, speaking and hearing. They look at each other, appreciating the beauty of each other's body.

Work out what these activities of sensual pleasuring are before you continue reading.

You can be like this couple—married lovers.

Let's spend a little time looking at how the couple in the Song of Songs enjoyed sensuality. Keep in mind that they enjoyed a delight in the *human body as a whole*, both male and female.

In each category, see if you can find other examples.

---

90   For example, if your wife shares with you that she thinks some part of her body (breasts, vulva) are ugly, you would be slow and gentle when including it in your lovemaking. If your husband shares that he has been worried about the size of his penis, or concerned that he could come too soon, you consider spending more time on the first stage activities before direct touching of his genitals.

Touch: The intimate sensuality of mutual touch is celebrated in the Song of Songs. Here are just a few examples.

She said: *My beloved is to me a sachet of myrrh resting between my breasts. My beloved is to me a cluster of henna blossoms from the vineyards of En Gedi* (1:13–14).

And he said: *Your navel is a rounded goblet that never lacks blended wine* (7:2). *Your stature is like that of the palm, and your breasts like clusters of fruit. I said, 'I will climb the palm tree; I will take hold of its fruit'* (7:7–8).

Kisses*:* The lovers also share and enjoy *breast touching and kissing.*

She said, *Let him kiss me with the kisses of his mouth— for your love is more delightful than wine* (1:2) and *His lips are like lilies dripping with myrrh* (5:13).

And he said, *Your lips are like a scarlet ribbon; your mouth is lovely. Your temples behind your veil are like the halves of a pomegranate* (4:3). *Your breasts are like two fawns, like twin fawns of a gazelle that browse among the lilies* (4:5). And *How delightful is your love, my sister, my bride! How much more pleasing is your love than wine, and the fragrance of your perfume more than any spice! Your lips drop sweetness as the honeycomb, my bride; milk and honey are under your tongue* (4:10–11).

Taste: The lovers bring the *sense of taste* into play.

She said, *Like an apple tree among the trees of the forest is my beloved among the young men. I delight to sit in his shade, and his fruit is sweet to my taste (2:3). His lips are like lilies dripping with myrrh (5:13). And May the wine go straight to my beloved, flowing gently over lips and teeth (7:9).*

Smell: And the enjoyment of *smell*.

She said, Pleasing is the fragrance of your perfumes; your name is like perfume poured out (1:3) and my perfume spread its fragrance. My beloved is to me a sachet of myrrh resting between my breasts. My beloved is to me a cluster of henna blossoms from the vineyards of En Gedi (1:12–14).

Throughout the book we see examples of what we, as therapists, encourage in couples' lovemaking:

Patience: The sexual intimacy between the couple is ramped up as we read on. However there is one important characteristic. Three times in the book we read the refrain 'do not arouse or awaken love until it so desires' (2:7; 3:5; 8:4). Wait, take it easy. And clear your mind and life of all the annoying 'little foxes' that distract you from concentrating on each other (2:15).

Mindfulness: Therapists call this focused attention on the pleasure the couple feel, a state of mindfulness. This mindfulness is rooted in their mutual love relationship.

You have stolen my heart, my sister, my bride; you have stolen my heart with one glance of your eyes, with one jewel of your necklace. How delightful is your love, my sister, my bride! How much more pleasing is your love than wine (4:9–10).

Physical intimacy: Although not explicit, there is a poetic description of bodily surrender (4:12–15) and a mutual pleasuring (5:1).

Covenant commitment in Christian marriage: Whereas the whole book is a wonderful poem about married sexual intimacy, Chapter 7 gives a climax of couple sex, with the expression of mutual bonding: *I belong to my beloved, and his desire is for me* (7:10). And a wonderful description of the intimacy that both satisfies and protects the relationship: *I am a wall, and my breasts are like towers. Thus I have become in his eyes like one bringing contentment* (8:10).

The three stages of sensual discovery

We now move to the physical intimacy activities. These activities enable you to move slowly through sensuality. Starting from the most basic of human contact (touch), you will slowly move through deepening levels of physical and emotional intimacy. Each takes 3–4 weeks. We recommend you take it slowly.

If you are uncomfortable with any activity, please stop and discuss it with each other. If after talking it over it still poses a problem, you may like to consider seeing a therapist or counsellor, or discuss it with a trusted older Christian couple.

Stage 1: Understanding and exploring the whole body

Stage 2: Exploring the whole body

Stage 3: Making love and having fun

Stage 1: Understanding and exploring the whole body

♡ **What is the goal of this activity?**
This first stage of the sensual discovery activity will:

- enable you as a couple to explore the sensual joy of sexual activity without the performance pressure of genital contact and intercourse
- encourage both partners to focus on the senses (touch, taste, smell and hearing) thereby setting new patterns of lovemaking and sensual other-focused pleasuring
- make time for honest and open communication and sharing on what gives each other pleasure
- build trust in the relationship
- increase chemicals like norepinephrine and dopamine in your brains. This will increase your intimacy and bonding.
- develop new sensual wiring in the brain. This serves different purposes in couples:
  1. In couples who have been celibate until marriage and have consciously blocked lust and fantasy, it enables the development of sensual thought patterns in the marriage relationship.
  2. In couples who have allowed their sexual intimacy to become patterned by the expectation that every act of intimacy must end with intercourse, it brings back the fun into non-intercourse intimacy.
  3. In those who have used pornography, it enables the development of images and thoughts that override images imprinted by porn, as well as building trust and honesty between the couple.

♥ **What is this Stage 1 activity?**
Stage 1 of sensual discovery involves touching each other's bodies in the way described. It is a slow and gentle reintroduction to the pleasure of sensuality and sexual intimacy.

We give you a schedule for three weeks, but you can be flexible.

Two basic rules

1. Refrain from touching the genital area. This also means that sexual intercourse should not take place at any time during this stage of the activity.
2. Stay in the moment. Know your body. Recognise and revel in the feelings and share these with your spouse. Be mindful of your feelings and those of your spouse. Remember that you are enjoying God's good gift to you both.

What the couple do

We will describe the activities using a hypothetical couple: Adam and Eve. You can be flexible in what you do and how you set the scene. Just keep to the two rules above.

♥ **Week 1, Session 1: Touching only**
Set aside about 30 minutes for the session. Set the scene as romantically as desired.

Fantasy scene setting

Individually, think about what *you* would consider to be the most romantic and sexy setting ever. Be as free and innovative as possible with your thinking. Share this with your partner. If you are initially embarrassed, write it down and email it to him/her.

The importance of touch

Touch is the most common and yet the most amazing sensation. Babies, children and adults are all emotionally affected by the lack of touch.

Eve's touching time

Eve and Adam have decided that Eve will be the one being touched in the first session.

Adam plans for this by setting the scene. He tries to create (at least some) of Eve's fantasy setting. He may keep this a surprise, or talk to her about it.

In this session, both partners undress completely, and Eve lies down on the bed and ensures that she is comfortable. Adam now starts to touch and stroke Eve's whole body from the top of her head to her toes, *omitting the genital area*. Halfway through the session Eve should turn over (if she started lying on her stomach, she turns over onto her back).

Adam's instructions

Think about what it feels like to touch Eve's body. Be mindful of the sensations. Does touching one part of her body feel different from another? How and why? What different textures can you feel? Is her body smoother or softer in some places than others? What parts do you enjoy caressing most?

Being mindful and staying in the moment will enable Adam to savour his thoughts, feelings and body sensations with an attitude of curiosity and non-judgement. He is building sensual thought patterns of Eve.

Eve will *tell him* how she feels. She may ask him to touch a particular part of her body. But it is important that Adam does not feel he *has to perform* in this stage. He must however be sensitive to her guidance.

In the Song of Songs, the lovers enjoy *speaking to each other* of how they feel. *Let me hear your voice*, he says, *for your voice is sweet* (2:14).

Make eye contact as much as possible. Enjoy the sight of Eve's body and her pleasure in your touch.

Eve's instructions

Relax. Be mindful of the sensations. Concentrate on the feelings. For a few minutes (5–10) Eve is to focus her thoughts and energy on sensation(s) of where Adam is touching her.

After this, Eve can direct him. She is to use affirming statements. For example, 'that feels nice, but I've often wondered what it would be like if you ... stroked my earlobes'. She could also direct his touch by putting her hand on his.

After the session

Later, after the session but while still undressed, Adam and Eve have a chat about what they were thinking and feeling, paying equal attention to the good and easy bits, as well as any areas that seemed difficult. Again, it is important that they both be affirmative and sensitive to each other.

Enjoy this session—make it *fun*, not an assignment.

♥ Week 1, Session 2: Touching only

Reverse the activity in Session 1 with Eve giving and Adam receiving the touch. Everything else is the same. Note: You may have the time and the desire for more sessions in this first week—if so, go for it! But keep the session structure as before.

♥ Week 2, Sessions 1 and 2: Mutual touching only

These two sessions are for *shared touch*. Adam and Eve *take turns* touching each other and talking about how it feels. Discuss what you have learned about your own body and that of your partner. Was there anything in particular that surprised you? Why?

Both *must remain mindful* of what they are feeling, both when giving and receiving touch. They may take short spells of giving and receiving. This is up to them.

♥ Week 3, Sessions 1, 2 and 3: Other sensations

This is when you ramp up the sensations! Remember, *no genital touch and no intercourse*. Adam and Eve continue as per the sessions last week, but start to *introduce more variation* into what they are doing.

Fantasy touch

Individually, think about what you enjoyed most about the touch only sessions. Think: maybe it would be lovely if Adam or Eve did _____ (fill in the blank). Be as free and innovative as possible with your thinking. Share this with your partner. If you are initially embarrassed, write it down and email it to him/her.

Now imagine what else you can do without genital contact and intercourse.

If you have been married for some time, think back to your dating days. What was it that turned you on then?

Think about:

- different types of touching, stroking and caressing such as kissing, nibbling and licking etc.

- different parts of the body where you can touch each other, such as palms, fingertips, the backs of the hands, lips and tongues, hair, eyelashes
- experiment with the feel of body lotions, massage oils and different fabrics (what does silk feel like against the skin? Or leather? Or velvet?)
- introduce food at this stage. Be innovative! Shared strawberries anyone? Whipped cream?
- sex toys. Remember a vibrator can be used on any part of the body.

These sessions are the most fun part of your lovemaking and will set sensuality patterns in your sexual repertoire that will last a lifetime of marriage.

Make sure the touch is mutual, and that the time taken for giving and receiving is roughly the same. Continue to be mindful and in the moment with regards to what you are thinking and feeling as you each give and receive.

After each session, while still nude, Adam and Eve must discuss how they felt and how easy or hard it was to keep mindful and stay in the moment.

Points to ponder
- Consider how you could set the scene for the exercises. Focus on what your partner said she/he would like.
- Remember that you have a lot of body other than the genitals! Even the most ticklish bits, like the feet, can be erotic areas when stimulated (kissed, sucked).
- You may like to take a bath together before the sessions. Try some bath oils or share a shower.

- The talking time is important. Talk and discuss: When you are the active partner, how does it feel to be touching your partner? What do you enjoy doing? What is less enjoyable? How do you sense your partner's pleasure? What are you thinking about and what, if anything, are you keeping to yourself?
- If you are the partner being touched, how does this feel? Are you relaxed? Afraid? Tense? Is your attention wandering? Are you wanting to be touched somewhere else? Do you feel able to tell your partner what you want?
- If you feel awkward about what you are doing, it might help to remember that many people do at this stage, but it's a stepping stone on the road to a more fulfilling sexual relationship. Share this awkwardness with your partner— laugh about it.
- What if one or both of you are aroused? That's fine. Discuss it and let it go. The man may have an ejaculation and the woman an orgasm. Talk about it, enjoy it, but don't use it in sexual intercourse.
- What if you want to have sex? Remind yourself of the *no sex* rule. The program aims to help you both find a pleasurable way of overcoming past problems, and to gain a more sensual and satisfying future together. This involves avoiding the performance pressure of intercourse for a period.
- Move to Stage 2 when you feel you are relaxed with each other and ready to introduce genital touch.

Stage 2: Exploring the whole body

♥ **What is the goal of this activity?**
   This second stage of the sensual discovery activity will:
* enable the couple to explore the sensual joy of sexual activity at a deeper level, without the performance pressure of intercourse
* encourage both to focus on the senses (touch, taste, smell and hearing) throughout the body, including the genitals
* encourage communication and sharing about what gives each pleasure, especially in the erotic areas of breasts and genitalia
* build a deepening trust in the relationship
* provide the opportunity for a deeper level of emotional intimacy.

♥ **What is this Stage 2 activity?**
   Stage 2 involves touching each other's bodies in the way described, exploring the whole body, including the breasts and genital area. Intercourse should not take place at any time during this stage of the program.

   We give you a three-week schedule, but you can be flexible.

Two basic rules
1. Refrain from sexual intercourse.
2. Stay in the moment. Know your body. Recognise and revel in the feelings and share these with your spouse. Be mindful of your feelings and those of your spouse. Remember that you are enjoying God's good gift to you both.

What the couple do

As in Stage 1, we will use the terms 'Adam' and 'Eve' to denote what each partner is to do. You can be flexible in what you do and how you set the scene. Just keep to the two basic rules.

♥ Week 1, Session 1: Breasts and chest

Set aside about 30 minutes for the session. Set the scene as romantically as desired.

Eve and Adam have decided that Eve will be the one being touched in the first session. Both undress completely, and Eve lies down on the bed and makes herself comfortable.

Adam's instructions

Adam now starts to touch and stroke her whole body from the top of her head to her toes, spending time especially on the breasts. Halfway through the session she should turn over (if she started lying on her stomach, she turns over onto her back).

Remember, you must continue with the same things you did before.

Think about what it feels like to touch Eve's body.

Be *mindful* of the sensations. Being mindful and staying in the moment will enable Adam to savour his thoughts, feelings and body sensations with an attitude of curiosity and non-judgement.

What different textures can he feel? Is her body smoother or softer in some places than others? What parts does he enjoy caressing most?

Eve will tell him how she feels. She may ask him to touch a particular part of her body. But it is important, as before, that Adam does not feel that he has to perform in this stage. He must however be sensitive to her guidance.

When she is on her back, make eye contact as much as possible.

Eve's instructions

Relax. Be *mindful* of the sensations. Concentrate on the feelings. For a few minutes (5–10) focus your thoughts and energy on sensation(s) of where Adam is touching you. Then share them with him.

After this, you can direct him. Use affirming statements. For example, 'that feels nice, but I've often wondered what it would be like if you ... (sucked on my nipples)'. You could also direct his touch by putting your hand on his.

After the session

Later, after the session and while still undressed, Adam and Eve have a chat about what they were thinking and feeling, paying equal attention to the good and easy bits, as well as any areas that seemed difficult. Again, it is important that they both be affirmative and sensitive to each other.

♥ Week 1, Session 2: Breasts and chest

Reverse the activity above with Eve giving and Adam receiving the touch. Everything else is the same. Remember, Adam has nipples too!

♥ Week 2, Sessions 1 and 2: Genital areas

When it feels comfortable for both of you to touch the breast and nipple areas, you can begin to include the genital areas. It will be helpful to use a sexual lubricant when you start to touch each other's genital areas. Dryness in this area is completely normal, just as skin elsewhere on our bodies often gets dry without moisturisers. Most couples find that using synthetic lubrication makes touch feel softer and more luxurious, especially in areas that have a lot of nerve endings such as the clitoris, penis and scrotum. We suggest you use a water-based lubricant like the Durex Play® range, Astroglide®, TLC® and Sylk®, or a silicone lubricant such as Silicone Moist®.

Session 1: Touching Adam

To touch a man's genitals, a good position to get into is the 'male comfortable' position. Here, the man lies on his back with his knees bent upwards while his partner leans back on pillows or other support, facing him. Start with gently touching his inner thighs and the testicles and build up to stroking, holding or rubbing the penis shaft, frenulum (the sensitive area near the tip) and glans (tip of the penis). Remember that the glans is particularly sensitive to touch, and be gentle. It doesn't matter if the penis is erect or flaccid during this exercise. You are not going to use it for intercourse.

The man may ejaculate or come—that's OK. Enjoy it. Discuss how it felt for you both.

Session 2: Touching Eve

To touch a female partner, you might find the 'armchair' position helpful. Here the woman sits in front of her partner, facing away and leans back against him. This allows the partner to stimulate the woman in a non-threatening way, and allows the woman to guide his hand towards what feels good. Start by gently touching and stroking the clitoral area, and move on to the rest of the vulva and the entrance to the vagina. If she is willing, Adam might go on to penetrate her vagina—slowly and gently—with one or more fingers. No intercourse yet please.

♥ Week 3, Sessions 1 and 2: Turning up the heat

Whoever is doing the stimulating, vary the speed, direction and degree of stimulation, and stop altogether from time to time (tease!) before restarting. In Adam, this will demonstrate how an erection can be lost and gained again quite easily (it is nothing to be worried about).

You can now up the stimuli. Be creative, share your fantasies. Think of fun ways to touch and stimulate the genitals. Use ways of pleasuring that you have used in Stage 1.

Sexual arousal is likely to occur for one or both of you, but this is a great opportunity to learn to enjoy sensual and sexual feelings for their own sake, without feeling the need to move on to penetrative sex. There is no rush. Intercourse is not the goal. Enjoy the journey.

Instead of working to create high arousal, just pay attention to any arousal you feel, enjoy it and let it go where it will. If either of you climaxes (has an orgasm), that's fine; if you don't, that's equally good. The aim is just to enjoy the experience of touching and being touched sexually, without feeling the need to work towards or 'achieve' orgasm. It is also a great way of reminding you that there is more to sex than penetration.

Adding oral stimulation

Oral techniques: When you have become comfortable with touching the nipples and genital areas, you might like to try some oral lovemaking, although this is not an essential part of the program. Some people shy away from this for fear that it is 'dirty', but assuming you have both taken care of general hygiene (by having a bath or shower), there is no reason why the genitals should be seen as any less 'clean' than any other part of the body.

Important point: For some people, oral sex is a very intense sexual activity. Spend time establishing mutual comfort in the activity. Any hint of coercion on the part of one partner could undo all the wonderful trust and pleasure you have built up so far.

For Adam: Oral sex on a woman is sometimes called cunnilingus. Use your tongue to gently kiss and lick your partner's clitoral area and vulva. Try this by itself, and then try it with your finger teasing the entrance to her vagina. You might also enjoy the opposite: putting your tongue inside the entrance to her vagina, perhaps while stimulating her clitoris with your finger. Experiment and see what you both enjoy!

For Eve: Oral sex on a man is sometimes called fellatio. Gently lick and kiss your partner's testicles and carry on to the penis, both the shaft and the tip, while continuing to stroke his testicles and the area around them. Many men enjoy having their penis sucked. If you take the penis too far into your mouth, however, it might activate the 'gag' reflex, so take it easy. If your partner gets very excited, he might want to ejaculate (come/cum/

climax). Some people are happy to let their partner come inside their mouth, whereas others are not keen on this. It's a good idea to discuss your preference with your partner beforehand, so you both know where you stand.

If you both enjoy simultaneous oral lovemaking, you might like to try the '69' position. This is where you give each other oral stimulation at the same time. As you might expect, you will need to lie with your heads at the opposite ends of the body to each other. Some couples do this with one partner lying above the other; others find it easier if you both lie on your side and face each other's genitals. Either way, take your time and enjoy the experience of giving and receiving pleasure at the same time. Soon you may be feeling more relaxed with each other and can consider kissing each other.

Points to ponder

- Consider how you could set the scene for the exercises.
- You may like to take a bath together before doing these activities.
- The talking time is important. Discuss: when you are the active partner, how does it feel to be touching your partner? What do you enjoy doing? What is less enjoyable? How do you sense your partner's pleasure? What are you thinking about, and what, if anything, are you keeping to yourself? If you are the partner being touched, how does this feel? Are you relaxed? Afraid? Tense? Is your attention wandering? Are you wanting to be touched somewhere else? Do you feel able to tell your partner what you want?
- If you feel awkward about what you are doing, it might help to remember that many people do at this stage, but

that it's a stepping stone on the road to a more fulfilling sexual relationship.

- What if one or both partners are aroused? He has an erection, she is wet and ready! That's fine. Discuss it and let it go. The man may have an ejaculation and the woman an orgasm. Talk about it, enjoy it, but don't use it.
- What if we want to have sex? Remind yourself of the *no sex* rule. The program aims to help you both find a pleasurable way of overcoming past problems, and to gain a more sensual and satisfying future together. If you slip up and have intercourse—well, it just means that you're ready for the next stage.

Stage 3: Making love and having fun

♥ What is the goal of this activity?

1. To enable the couple to explore the sensual joy of having sexual intercourse in a new and exciting way.

2. Encourage both to focus on the senses (touch, taste, smell and hearing) throughout the body, including the genitals, especially during intercourse.

3. To encourage communication and sharing about what gives each partner pleasure, especially just before, during and after the intercourse experience.

4. To build trust in the relationship.

Stage 3 of sensual discovery involves sexual intercourse. It will enable you to see this experience of coupling as a special experience, to bring to bear on it all the exercises you have done in Stages 1 and 2.

Important point: If you are using a contraceptive, especially a condom, discuss it before you start and plan how you can introduce the use in a fun and arousing way.

It might be tempting to think 'OK, back to normal', but this would be a missed opportunity. I want you to apply everything you've learned so far and discover new things about sexual intercourse, not just fall back on doing what you've always done.

This is an opportunity for both of you to experience and appreciate intercourse in a different way. I want to encourage you to reframe your thinking:

- Move your thinking away from sexual intercourse as an 'in and out—friction and thrusting' activity.
- Be there in the moment (the old exercise of mindfulness). You will learn the exquisite and intimate feeling of just being without doing. Learning this can greatly increase both physical sensation and emotional closeness.
- You have learned to enjoy the journey of non-intercourse sexual intimacy in Stages 1 and 2. Continue with these. Don't stress on the end point of intercourse. Don't worry if you don't feel like intercourse every time. Enjoy the journey from first touch to intercourse.
- If either one of you has a sexual problem (for example, erectile failure or rapid ejaculation in the male or vaginismus in the female) take this stage slowly and gently.

What to do

To get started, choose one of the two sexual positions described. If the position you had been using before has been the man on top and lying in bed, forget this for a while. Try something new.

1. Woman above position

For Eve: Kneel astride your partner, facing him. The woman gently guides his penis slowly into her vagina. In this position, she is able to control the depth of penetration: if she leans forward with her chest close to his, penetration will be quite shallow, whereas if she sits upright or leans back a little, penetration will be deeper.

Try both variations and see what you both enjoy most. Think of the penis as yours to play with, explore and enjoy. It will also be easy in this position to kiss, maintain good eye contact and for either of you to stroke your clitoris and breasts. You might also like to try reaching round behind you and very gently stroking your partner's testicles (although this is probably not a good idea if you are trying to overcome rapid ejaculation).

'Woman above' is a very useful position for helping to solve almost any kind of sexual problem. It allows the man with erectile or ejaculatory difficulties to relax and achieve a degree of penetration without having to manoeuvre into position. For a woman who has difficulty allowing penetration or achieving orgasm, it gives the opportunity to move towards these goals at her own pace.

2. The scissor position

For Adam: In this position, the man lies on his side and the woman lies on her back next to him at an angle of approximately 45 degrees. She bends her knees up towards her tummy and places her calves over his hips, so that they are resting on his bottom. The entrance to her vagina should be snugly against his pelvis.

Gently insert your penis into your partner's vagina (your partner may need to bend her legs back a little further to assist penetration and ensure that your pelvises are comfortably together). A variation is to try having one of your partner's legs between yours as pictured on page 226. This position gives good access to the woman's clitoris and breasts (although it does make kissing and eye contact a bit more difficult because of the angle you are lying at).

'Scissors' is very relaxing, and is a good position if you are both tired after a long day! Women need to be adequately aroused and relaxed before penetration begins. Men often assume women are ready long before they are, so we suggest you agree between you that Eve will decide when she is ready to be penetrated, and let Adam know. Similarly, Adam will need an adequate erection for penetration, but this does not mean he has to be extremely hard and erect. Through experience and by using a lubricant, you will learn that 'adequate' may mean much less erect than you might have previously thought was necessary!

For either position:

- Set the scene as you have done in previous sessions, and spend some time enjoying each other's bodies, drawing on everything you have learned in Stages 1 and 2.
- When you both feel ready, and as a part of your love-play, put plenty of lubricant on the penis and at the entrance to the vagina. Or use saliva as a lubricant.
- Relax and breathe slowly, then move into whichever of the two positions you have chosen.
- Start to penetrate very slowly (really, we do mean a millimetre at a time!). Make it slow and sensuous, so that each of you really has time to luxuriate in the sensations and feelings it creates.
- When the man is inside as far as is comfortable for both of you, stop and keep still for a few moments. Breathe deeply and enjoy the feeling of penetrating and being penetrated. Imagine the vagina welcoming, embracing and containing the penis. Do not worry about the firmness of the man's erection, but instead relax and enjoy each other's attention.
- While you do this, you may enjoy making eye contact with each other, telling each other your feelings and what you

are experiencing, and stroking each other's bodies. The woman may enjoy touching her own clitoris or breasts to enhance her arousal, or asking Adam to do this.

- When you are ready (or if the penis starts to become soft), make some gentle movements of the penis and vagina backwards and forwards or up and down (depending on which position you are trying), then pause again. If the penis slips out of the vagina at any time, don't worry—just slip it gently back in. If it is not hard enough to penetrate again, one of you can spend some time pleasuring the penis (as you learned in Stage 2) before trying again.

The two positions described are especially good for this kind of lovemaking, but feel free to experiment with other positions.

Relax and enjoy the experience of penetration in a new way. If either or both of you want to go on to climax, either during or after this exercise, that's OK, but it is certainly not a requirement. Rather, the idea is to bring the sensations in your genitals fully into your conscious awareness, and discover that intercourse isn't all (or even mostly) about vigorous movement or thrusting. Tiny movements can be incredibly pleasurable. Sometimes less is more: the less movement and exertion, the more sensitivity you both experience. If you do not climax, this does not mean the sex has been a waste of time. Sex without orgasms can be very satisfying for both men and women.

We hope that, by the end of the Sensual Discovery Pathway you will be on the road to allaying the sexual concerns you have. And more than that, you will also have discovered (if you didn't know already) that there is a lot more to sexual enjoyment for both partners than thrusting, orgasm and ejaculation!

This is the last of the three stages of sensual exercises. Just because you have graduated at Stage 3 does not mean you should not go back occasionally to Stages 1 and 2.

For the more adventurous

Here are some additional sex positions you may like to experiment with. Always remember that any new or novel activity must be one that is agreed on by both of you. There must *never be even a hint of coercion* in a sexual relationship.

Variations on the male on top position
1. The classic

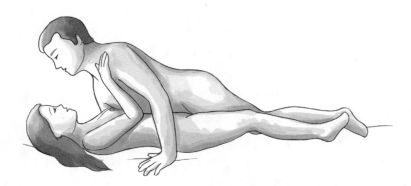

Eve lies with her legs open, with cushions placed under her bottom to tilt her up for deeper penetration. Adam lies on top of her and enters her, taking his weight on his arms and controlling the movements. This intimate position is both stimulating and relaxing, allowing the couple to embrace and caress each other. Eve's movements are limited but her hands are free to stroke her partner.

2. The female knee wrap

She lies on her back with her legs open, while he lies between her legs and enters her. She then wraps her legs around him and uses her feet to guide him by putting gentle pressure on his buttocks using her feet. Both have their hands free to touch and caress each other, and the woman can stroke her partner's back and bottom. This is a very simple position for intimate lovemaking.

3. Female legs together

She lies on her back, stretches her legs out and holds onto the bedposts above her head. She keeps her legs together as he enters her with his thighs outside hers. With every thrust the pressure of her thighs intensifies the penetration effect and provides for a natural stimulation of the clitoris.

Variations of the female on top
4. Female-controlled entry

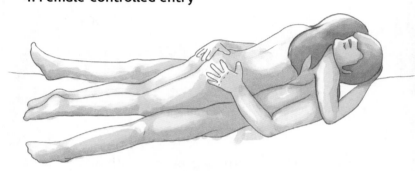

He lies down on the bed with his legs stretched out. She then gets on top of him and lets him enter her. As he does so, she stretches her legs out straight behind her and starts to move back and forth as fast or as slow as she likes. It's a great position for full body contact, kissing and touching throughout. Importantly, it gives the woman control over how far she would like penetration.

5. Female slide

He is on his back, the woman lies on top with her legs together. While he penetrates her she begins to rub up and down his body. The slide sex position is pretty easy to master. Use a massage oil to make the experience even more sensuous.

Posterior entry
These two positions are good to use when the woman is pregnant.

6. Both kneeling

She's on all fours. In order to hold her balance, she shifts her weight off her hands back towards her partner—she can use a rocking motion to get the rhythm she wants. He kneels directly behind her and holds her hips firmly to control the thrusts. There is no pressure on the abdomen or breasts and the movement can be controlled by the woman.

7. Both in bed

She curls up on her side, knees drawn up and the man spoons her from behind. Penetration is fairly easy from this position and the man can reach around to play with her breasts or genitals. If the knees are less drawn in, it will be more comfortable for a growing bump.

Help if the man is disabled
8. Male seated

He sits comfortably on a chair; the woman sits down on him facing forwards so she's straddling him. As long as her feet are touching the ground she can bounce up and down on him gently. This is a good position if the man has a weakness in his thighs or legs.

Appendix 3:
How do I love thee?

♥ **What is the goal of this activity?**
This activity that follows gives you the opportunity to learn the sensual preferences of your partner. It also gives a safe place to practise your communication skills.

Part 1 (15 minutes)
Complete the questionnaire on page 235 *individually*. (You may wish to photocopy the page or write your answers on a separate sheet of paper.)

Each statement is in *two* parts. The column on the left is *your personal response*. The one on the right is *how you think your spouse would respond*.

Part 2 (no time limit)
You now have time as a couple to discuss the responses.

1. Exchange the questionnaires. Please keep calm as you read your spouse's responses.
2. Compare what you have said was your personal response to each item with what your spouse thought your response would be.
3. Find one area where there is a difference.
4. Discuss the differences between your perceptions and those of your spouse.

When doing this, listen to what your spouse has to say. It helps to rephrase what has been said to confirm that you correctly heard and understood what he/she said. One way is to use the phrase 'what I hear you say is ...' and allow the other person to confirm or clarify their view.

Don't interrupt the other person, even if you feel upset. Wait until he/she has finished and then express your feelings with a phrase like, 'what you said makes me feel ... (sad, upset, annoyed, etc.) because ...' Then listen to his/her response and reasons.

5. Take turns choosing and discussing one or more questions.

How do I love thee?

The activity

Your personal response	How do you think your spouse would respond?
When we are making love, it feels good when you …	When we are making love, I think you really enjoy it when I …
What I most enjoy about our lovemaking is …	What I think you most enjoy about our lovemaking is …
When we are making love, I would rather you didn't …	When we are making love, I get the feeling that you would rather I didn't …
I would like to … in our lovemaking.	I think you would like to … in our lovemaking.
My favourite time of the day to make love is …	I think your favourite time of the day to make love is …
My favourite place to make love is …	I think your favourite place to make love is …

Appendix 4:
Advice to a porn user

The information here is not a treatment program. Nor is it a replacement for formal counselling. It is a set of guidelines for those who think they have a problem with pornography.

It doesn't matter if you are an occasional or opportunistic user, a compulsive viewer/reader, or addicted to porn. If it causes you distress and affects your spouse, family and life in general, you must do something to stop this perverted use of God's gift of sex.

The six-step plan
Step 1. Stop!

Keep in mind that pornography is not only internet-based. It could be images, videos, erotic literature or television programs.

You must take responsibility. Your spouse is your partner in the process. She/he is not responsible for your porn use; nor can she/he police your activities.

This complete withdrawal will feel painful. Remember Christ's words:

> *And if your eye causes you to stumble, pluck it out. It is better for you to enter the kingdom of God with one eye than to have two eyes and be thrown into hell …*
> (Mark 9:47)

Even the Apostle Paul struggled to keep his body in check!

> *No, I strike a blow to my body and make it my slave so that after I have preached to others, I myself will not be disqualified for the prize.* (1 Corinthians 9:27)

As a child of the divine God you are free and empowered to fight this sin. (See Romans 6:1–11. Verse 11 says *count yourselves dead to sin but alive to God in Christ Jesus.*)

Accountability software programs may not stop your desire for porn, but it can be a deterrent. Get one installed. We recommend the Covenant Eyes accountability software[91] or X3watch[92].

So you have decided to stop, and you really want to. But, how do you do it?

Step 2: Find yourself accountability mentors

You must firstly *acknowledge* that pornography is a sexual sin and not worthy of a Christlike lifestyle. You should then bring yourself to *confess* this. You need to follow the admonition of James and confess sins rather than hiding them. As a married man, this confession needs to be made to your wife and to another wiser, older Christian man. Similarly, if you are a married woman you need to confess to your husband and an older, wiser Christian woman.

> *Therefore confess your sins to each other and pray for each other so that you may be healed. The prayer of a righteous person is powerful and effective.* (James 5:16)

---

91   http://www.covenanteyes.com/
92   http://www.x3watch.com/

Remember that as a Christian you live under God's grace. Christ died in our place, bearing our guilt, so that there is now no condemnation for those who are in Christ Jesus (Romans 8:1). You may have been a porn user, adulterer or addicted to lustful fantasy. Jesus died for you, and if you are now in Christ Jesus there is no condemnation. As 1 Corinthians 6:9–11 says, *Do not be deceived: Neither the sexually immoral nor idolaters nor adulterers nor men who have sex with men nor thieves nor the greedy nor drunkards nor slanderers nor swindlers will inherit the kingdom of God. And that is what some of you were. But you were washed, you were sanctified, you were justified in the name of the Lord Jesus Christ and by the Spirit of our God.* Hang on to this truth.

Now, find yourself accountability mentors. These are people who can 'walk the talk' with you as you heal.

> *But encourage one another daily, as long as it is called 'Today', so that none of you may be hardened by sin's deceitfulness.* (Hebrews 3:13)

What characteristics should these mentors have?

- It is best you have at least three, preferably older, people (males if you are male and female if you are female). This increases the likelihood of one of them being available at any time you need help.
- They should be committed Christians.
- It would be good if at least one of these people has struggled with some form of sexual sin himself/herself.
- They should be willing and available for you to text, email or call at *any* time.

How should it work?

1. You text or call when you feel the urge to watch pornography.
2. They talk you through the difficulty and pray with you.
3. If you don't call them after a set period, they call/text to ask how you're going.
4. You call them if you slip and they pray and talk you through that too.
5. They receive the results of your web-browsing history.
6. You meet regularly either one on one or as a group to talk, read the Bible and pray.

Note: Your spouse cannot be your 'accountability partner' or police your activities.

Step 3: Keep a journal

Often there are particular feelings, emotions or times of the day that trigger the desire to watch pornography. You need to identify these triggers or reasons for porn use.

Keeping a journal is a good way to do this.

Work out replacement activities: Find some activity that you can do to replace pornography at the moment when you feel the desire to use it. Something active such as a run or a gym workout will help by releasing a whole lot of feel-good hormones.

Write these details down in your journal. Think of others. Discuss this with your mentors.

Step 4: Cover yourself with grace

Pray and read the Bible; do not neglect this.

Put on the full armour of God, so that you can take your stand against the devil's schemes. For our struggle is not against flesh and blood, but against the rulers, against the authorities, against the powers of this dark world and against the spiritual forces of evil in the heavenly realms. Therefore put on the full armour of God, so that when the day of evil comes, you may be able to stand your ground, and after you have done everything, to stand. Stand firm then, with the belt of truth buckled round your waist, with the breastplate of righteousness in place, and with your feet fitted with the readiness that comes from the gospel of peace. In addition to all this, take up the shield of faith, with which you can extinguish all the flaming arrows of the evil one. Take the helmet of salvation and the sword of the Spirit, which is the word of God. (Ephesians 5:11–17)

Step 5: Reflect on your progress and reward yourself

Have you been off pornography use for a week? A month? Six months? Reward yourself! Do something you enjoy. If you are married, do it with your spouse.

Step 6: Requesting professional help

If you have tried the above steps and find that you are still caught in the habit, you need professional help. There is no shame in asking for assistance.

Your pastor or your doctor should be the first person you talk to.

Building intimacy after porn

The final goal for a couple is more than 'quitting pornography'. Stopping porn use is of course admirable, but it leaves a void. Remember the parable Jesus gave about throwing out one evil and not replacing it with godliness?

> *When an impure spirit comes out of a person, it goes through arid places seeking rest and does not find it. Then it says, 'I will return to the house I left'. When it arrives, it finds the house unoccupied, swept clean and put in order. Then it goes and takes with it seven other spirits more wicked than itself, and they go in and live there. And the final condition of that person is worse than the first. That is how it will be with this wicked generation.* (Matthew 12:43–45)

You need to replace the void that porn leaves in your mind. Fill your mind with good and pure thoughts (Philippians 4:8), and re-establish true intimacy with your spouse. Rewire your desire and sensuality circuits. Reclaim what pornography has stolen from your marriage.

This may take time and effort. There is forgiveness and grace involved. Don't be afraid to ask for help as a couple. Remember, nothing can separate you from the love of God.

> *Who shall separate us from the love of Christ? Shall trouble or hardship or persecution or famine or nakedness or danger or sword? As it is written: 'For your sake we face death all day long; we are considered as sheep to be slaughtered'. No, in all these things we are more than conquerors through him who loved us. For I am convinced that neither death nor life, neither angels*

nor demons, neither the present nor the future, nor any powers, neither height nor depth, nor anything else in all creation, will be able to separate us from the love of God that is in Christ Jesus our Lord. (Romans 8:35–39)

In marriage, you will need to re-establish couple intimacy patterns. Your therapist (if you are seeing one) may recommend a series of sensuality exercises for you to do as a couple. These will:

1. enable you and your spouse as a couple to explore the sensual joy of sexual activity without the performance pressure of genital contact and intercourse
2. encourage both partners to focus on the senses (touch, taste, smell and hearing) thereby setting new patterns of lovemaking and sensual other-focused pleasuring
3. make time for honest and open communication and sharing on what gives each pleasure
4. build trust in the relationship
5. increase chemicals like norepinephrine and dopamine in your brain in the context of your marriage relationship. This will increase your intimacy and bonding.
6. develop new sensual wiring in the brain. The development of images and thoughts of your couple intimacy will slowly override images imprinted by porn.

You may find the activities in Appendix 2 useful.

The use of pornography rewires the brain. Rewiring the brain to God's pattern of other-focused, loving sexual activity in marriage takes time and effort. However, it is worth it. Don't be ashamed to confess and ask for help from your church community and seek professional counselling if you need it.

Appendix 5:
Bibliography

Ash, C 2003, *Marriage: Sex in the Service of God*, InterVarsity Press, Nottingham.

Ash, C 2007, *Married for God: Making Your Marriage the Best It Can Be*, InterVarsity Press, Nottingham.

Bird, M & Preece, G 2012, *Sexegesis: An Evangelical Response to Five Uneasy Pieces on Homosexuality*, Anglican Press Australia, Sydney.

Brandon, G 2009, *Just Sex: Is it Ever Just Sex?*, InterVarsity Press, Nottingham.

Clarke, A & Clark, G 2001, *One Flesh: A Practical Guide to Honeymoon Sex and Beyond*, Matthias Media, Sydney.

Davidson, RM 2007, *Flame of Yahweh: Sexuality in the Old Testament*, Hendrickson, Massachusetts.

Freitas, D 2008, *Sex and the Soul: Juggling Sexuality, Spirituality, Romance, and Religion on America's College Campuses*, Oxford University Press, New York.

Grenz, SJ 1997, *Sexual Ethics: An Evangelical Perspective*, Westminster John Knox Press, Louisville.

Hollinger, DP 2009, *The Meaning Of Sex: Christian Ethics and the Moral Life*, Baker Academic, Grand Rapids.

Keller, T & Keller, K 2011, *The Meaning of Marriage: Facing the Complexities of Commitment with the Wisdom of God*, Dutton, New York.

Köstenberger, AJ 2004, *God, Marriage, and Family: Rebuilding the Biblical Foundation*, Crossway, Wheaton.

Kuehne, D 2009, *Sex and the iWorld*, Baker Academic, Grand Rapids.

Leman, K 2008, *Sheet Music: Uncovering the Secrets of Sexual Intimacy in Marriage*, Tyndale House Publishers, Carol Stream.

Payne, T & Jensen, PD 1998, *Pure Sex*, Matthias Media, Sydney.

Piper, J 2009, *This Momentary Marriage: A Parable of Permanence*, Crossway Books, Wheaton.

Piper, J & Grudem, W (eds) 2006, *Recovering Biblical Manhood and Womanhood: A Response to Evangelical Feminism*, Crossway Books, Wheaton.

Piper, J & Taylor, J (eds) 2005, *Sex and the Supremacy of Christ*, Crossway Books, Wheaton.

Regnerus, M & Uecker, J 2011, *Premarital Sex in America: How Young Americans Meet, Mate, and Think about Marrying*, Oxford University Press, USA.

Robertson, OP 2002, *The Genesis of Sex: Sexual Relationships in the First Book of the Bible*, Presbyterian & Reformed, Philipsberg.

Simon, C 2012, *Bringing Sex into Focus: The Quest for Sexual Intimacy*, InterVarsity Press, Nottingham.

Smith, C 2012, *God's Good Design: What the Bible says about Men and Women*, Matthias Media, Sydney.

Struthers, W 2009, *Wired for Intimacy: How Pornography Hijacks the Male Brain*, InterVarsity Press, Nottingham.

Tankard-Reist, M & Bray, A (eds) 2011, *Big Porn Inc: Exposing the Harms of the Global Pornography Industry*, Spinifex Press, North Melbourne.

Wheat, E & Wheat, G 2010, *Intended for Pleasure*, 4th edition, Revell, Ada.

Winner, LF 2005, *Real Sex: The Naked Truth about Chastity*, Think Books, London.